THE VISUAL DICTIONARY *of*
BUILDINGS

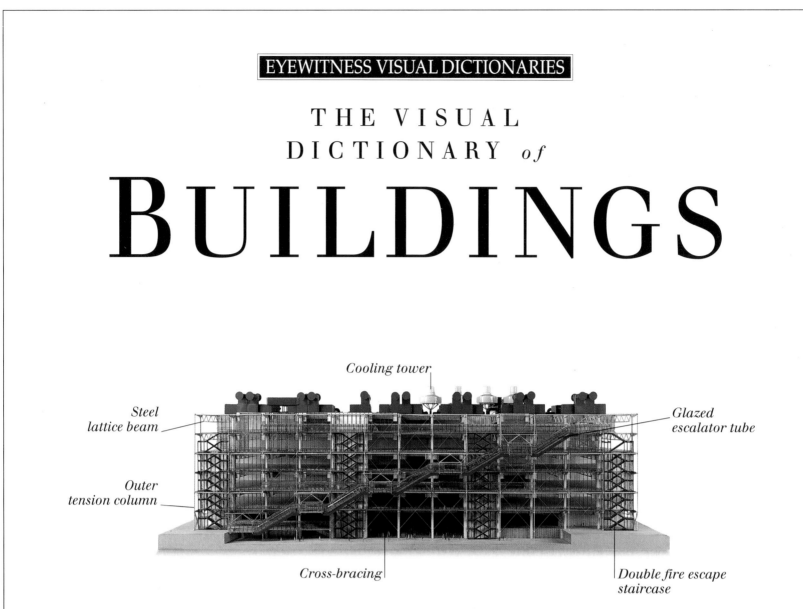

Cooling tower

Steel
lattice beam

Glazed
escalator tube

Outer
tension column

Cross-bracing

Double fire escape
staircase

PRINCIPAL FACADE, CENTRE GEORGES POMPIDOU, PARIS, FRANCE, 1977

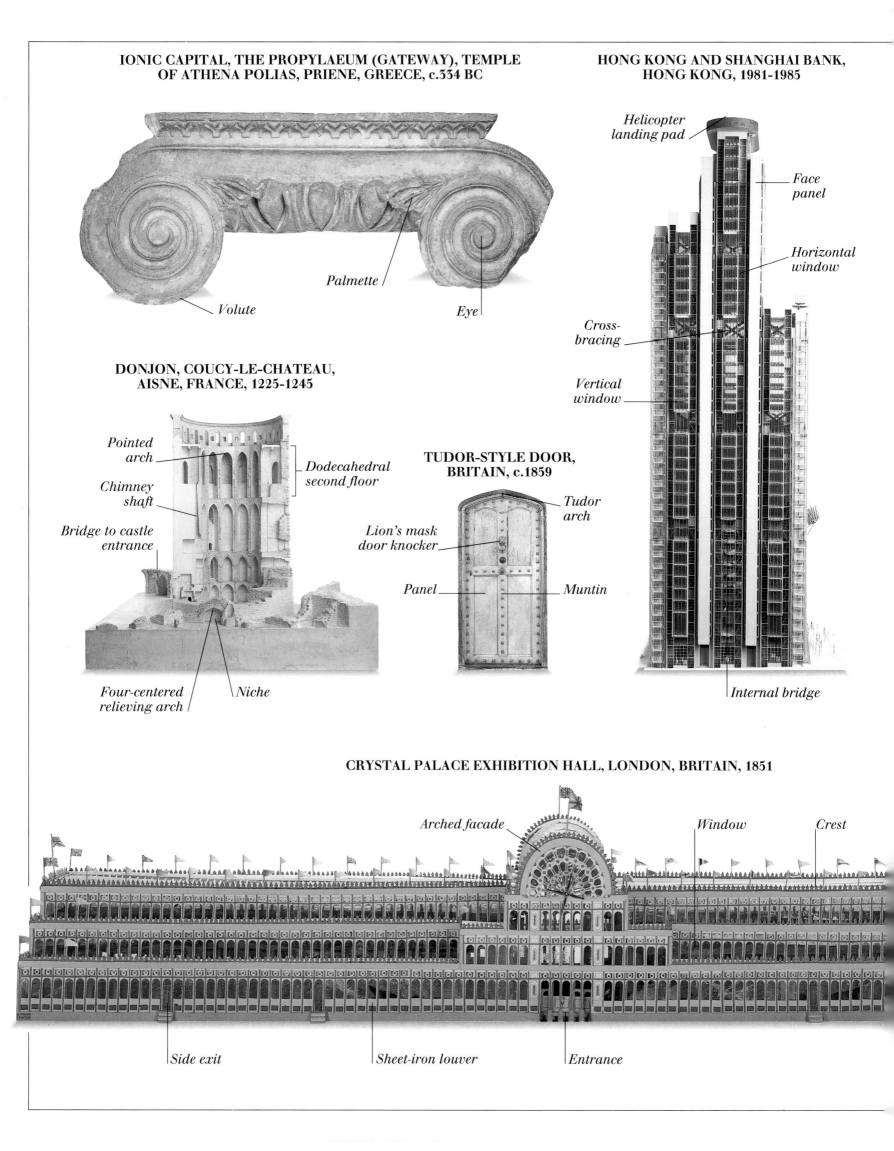

IONIC CAPITAL, THE PROPYLAEUM (GATEWAY), TEMPLE OF ATHENA POLIAS, PRIENE, GREECE, c.334 BC

Palmette

Volute

Eye

HONG KONG AND SHANGHAI BANK, HONG KONG, 1981-1985

Helicopter landing pad

Face panel

Horizontal window

Cross-bracing

Vertical window

Internal bridge

DONJON, COUCY-LE-CHATEAU, AISNE, FRANCE, 1225-1245

Pointed arch

Chimney shaft

Bridge to castle entrance

Dodecahedral second floor

Four-centered relieving arch

Niche

TUDOR-STYLE DOOR, BRITAIN, c.1859

Tudor arch

Lion's mask door knocker

Panel

Muntin

CRYSTAL PALACE EXHIBITION HALL, LONDON, BRITAIN, 1851

Arched facade

Window

Crest

Side exit

Sheet-iron louver

Entrance

EYEWITNESS VISUAL DICTIONARIES

THE VISUAL DICTIONARY *of*
BUILDINGS

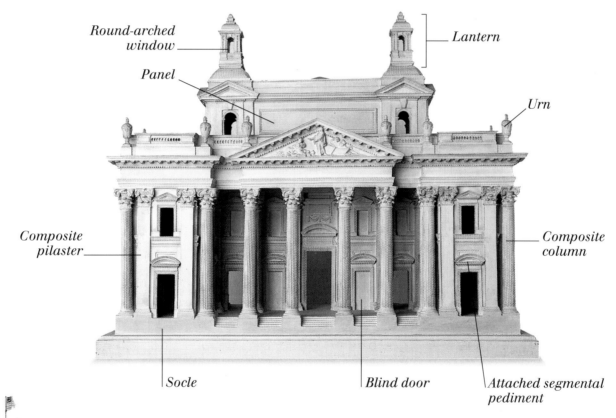

Round-arched window

Panel

Lantern

Urn

Composite pilaster

Composite column

Socle

Blind door

Attached segmental pediment

PROPOSED FACADE, THE MADELEINE, PARIS, FRANCE, 1764

DK

DORLING KINDERSLEY, INC.

NEW YORK

A DORLING KINDERSLEY BOOK

PROJECT ART EDITOR NICOLA LIDDIARD
DESIGNER PAUL CALVER

PROJECT EDITOR ROGER TRITTON
EDITOR FIONA COURTENAY-THOMPSON
CONSULTANT EDITOR ALEXANDRA KENNEDY

MANAGING ART EDITOR STEPHEN KNOWLDEN
SENIOR EDITOR MARTYN PAGE
MANAGING EDITOR RUTH MIDGLEY
U.S. EDITOR CHARLES A. WILLS

PHOTOGRAPHY TIM RIDLEY, ANDY CRAWFORD
ILLUSTRATIONS JOHN WOODCOCK, SIMONE END, KATHLEEN MCDOUGALL

PRODUCTION HILARY STEPHENS

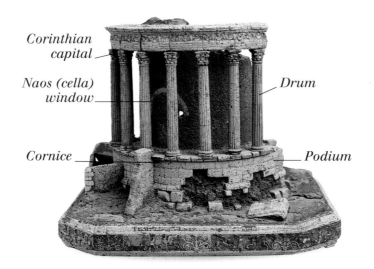

Corinthian capital

Naos (cella) window

Drum

Cornice

Podium

TEMPLE OF VESTA, TIVOLI, ITALY, c.80 BC

FIRST AMERICAN EDITION, 1992

10 9 8 7 6 5 4 3 2 1

DORLING KINDERSLEY INC., 232 MADISON AVENUE,
NEW YORK, NEW YORK 10016

COPYRIGHT © 1992 DORLING KINDERSLEY LIMITED, LONDON

LIBRARY OF CONGRESS CATALOGING-IN-PUBLICATION DATA

EYEWITNESS VISUAL DICTIONARY OF BUILDINGS. — 1ST AMERICAN ED.
p. cm. — (THE EYEWITNESS VISUAL DICTIONARIES)
INCLUDES INDEX.
SUMMARY: LABELED ILLUSTRATIONS WITH EXPLANATORY TEXT DEPICT
HISTORICAL AND CONTEMPORARY STRUCTURES, ARCHITECTURAL ELEMENTS, AND
BUILDING COMPONENTS FROM ANCIENT TIMES TO THE PRESENT.
ISBN 1–56458–102–0
1. ARCHITECTURE—DICTIONARIES. 2. DECORATION AND ORNAMENT,
ARCHITECTURAL—DICTIONARIES. [1. ARCHITECTURE. 2. DECORATION AND
ORNAMENT, ARCHITECTURAL. 3. BUILDINGS.] I. DORLING KINDERSLEY,
INC. II. SERIES.
NA31.E97 1992
720'.3—dc20   92–7673
                                                      CIP
                                                      AC

REPRODUCED BY COLOURSCAN, SINGAPORE
PRINTED AND BOUND IN ITALY BY ARNOLDO MONDADORI, VERONA

Contents

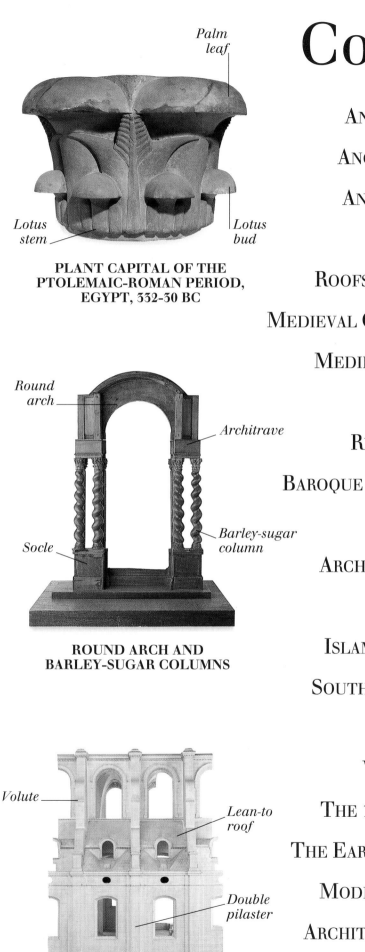

Palm leaf

Lotus stem

Lotus bud

PLANT CAPITAL OF THE PTOLEMAIC-ROMAN PERIOD, EGYPT, 332-30 BC

Round arch

Architrave

Socle

Barley-sugar column

ROUND ARCH AND BARLEY-SUGAR COLUMNS

Volute

Lean-to roof

Double pilaster

CHURCH OF ST. PAUL-ST. LOUIS, PARIS, FRANCE, FROM 1627

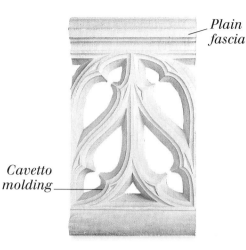

Plain fascia

Cavetto molding

GOTHIC CURVILINEAR (FLOWING) TRACERY

Circular molding

VICTORIAN MOLDED BRICK

Arris

"RUBBER" (SOFT, EASILY-SPLIT) BRICK

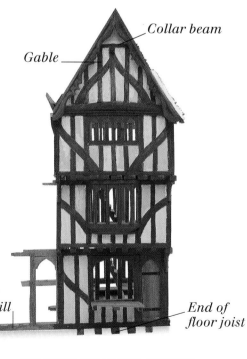

Collar beam

Gable

Sill

End of floor joist

TIMBER-FRAMED HOUSE, BRITAIN, c.1450

Ancient Egypt

THE CIVILIZATION OF THE ANCIENT EGYPTIANS (which lasted from about 3100 BC until it was finally absorbed into the Roman empire in 30 BC) is famous for its temples and tombs. Egyptian temples were often huge and geometric, like the Temple of Amon-Re (below and right). They were usually decorated with hieroglyphs (sacred characters used for picture writing) and painted reliefs depicting gods, Pharaohs (kings), and queens. Tombs were particularly important to the Egyptians, who believed that the dead were resurrected in the afterlife. The tombs were often decorated—as, for example, the surround of the false door opposite— in order to give comfort to the dead. The best-known ancient Egyptian tombs are the pyramids (see pp. 58-59), which were designed to symbolize the rays of the sun. Many of the architectural forms used by the ancient Egyptians were later adopted by other civilizations. For example, columns and capitals were later used by the ancient Greeks (see pp. 8-9) and ancient Romans (see pp. 10-11).

SIDE VIEW OF HYPOSTYLE HALL, TEMPLE OF AMON-RE, KARNAK, EGYPT, c.1290 BC

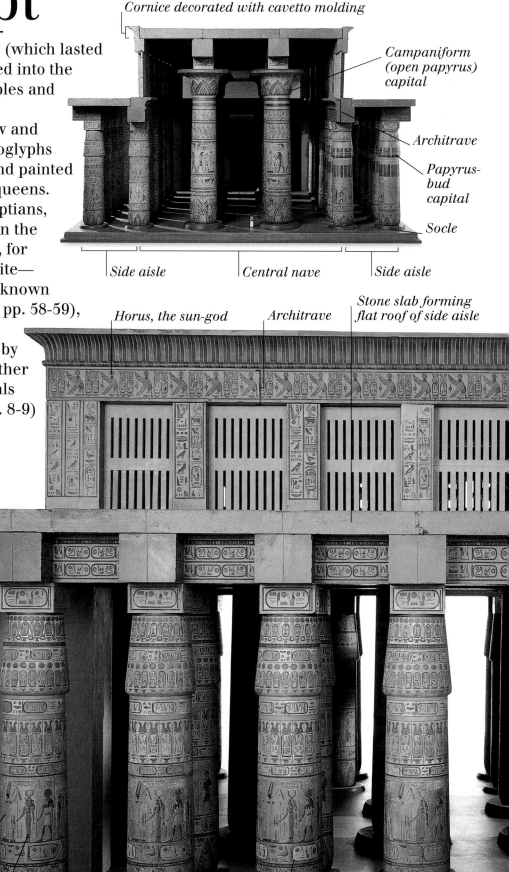

FRONT VIEW OF HYPOSTYLE HALL, TEMPLE OF AMON-RE

Cornice decorated with cavetto molding

Campaniform (open papyrus) capital

Architrave

Papyrus-bud capital

Socle

Side aisle

Central nave

Side aisle

Horus, the sun-god

Architrave

Stone slab forming flat roof of side aisle

Kepresh crown with disc

Chons, the moon-god

Amon-Re, king of the gods

Hathor, the sky-goddess

Papyrus motif

Cartouche (oval border) containing the titles of the Pharaoh (king)

Socle

Aisle running north–south

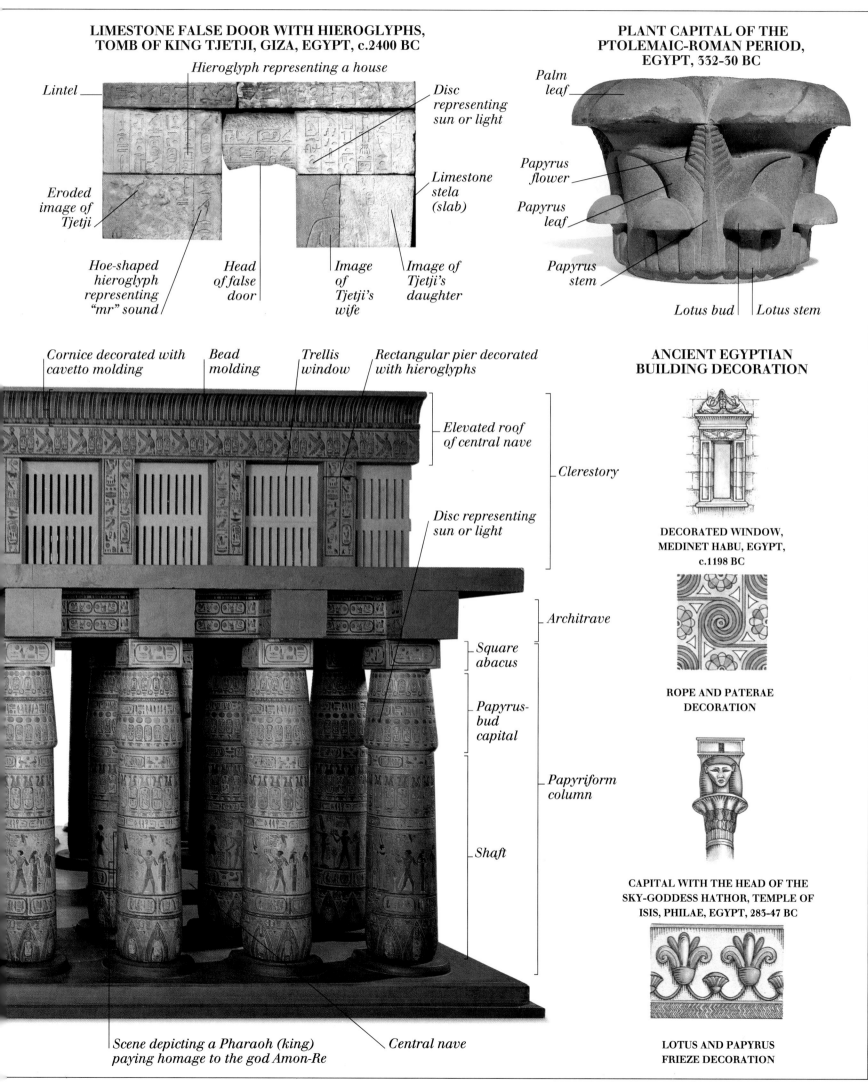

**LIMESTONE FALSE DOOR WITH HIEROGLYPHS,
TOMB OF KING TJETJI, GIZA, EGYPT, c.2400 BC**

Hieroglyph representing a house

Lintel

Disc representing sun or light

Eroded image of Tjetji

Limestone stela (slab)

Hoe-shaped hieroglyph representing "mr" sound

Head of false door

Image of Tjetji's wife

Image of Tjetji's daughter

**PLANT CAPITAL OF THE
PTOLEMAIC-ROMAN PERIOD,
EGYPT, 332-30 BC**

Palm leaf

Papyrus flower

Papyrus leaf

Papyrus stem

Lotus bud

Lotus stem

Cornice decorated with cavetto molding

Bead molding

Trellis window

Rectangular pier decorated with hieroglyphs

Elevated roof of central nave

Clerestory

Disc representing sun or light

Architrave

Square abacus

Papyrus-bud capital

Papyriform column

Shaft

Scene depicting a Pharaoh (king) paying homage to the god Amon-Re

Central nave

**ANCIENT EGYPTIAN
BUILDING DECORATION**

**DECORATED WINDOW,
MEDINET HABU, EGYPT,
c.1198 BC**

**ROPE AND PATERAE
DECORATION**

**CAPITAL WITH THE HEAD OF THE
SKY-GODDESS HATHOR, TEMPLE OF
ISIS, PHILAE, EGYPT, 283-47 BC**

**LOTUS AND PAPYRUS
FRIEZE DECORATION**

Ancient Greece

THE CLASSICAL TEMPLES OF ANCIENT GREECE were built according to the belief that certain forms and proportions were pleasing to the gods. There were three main Ancient Greek architectural orders (styles), which can be distinguished by the decoration and proportions of their columns, capitals (column tops), and entablatures (structures resting on the capitals). The oldest is the Doric order, which dates from the seventh century BC and was used mainly on the Greek mainland and in the western colonies, such as Sicily and southern Italy. The Temple of Neptune, shown here, is a classic example of this order. It is hypaethral (roofless) and peripteral (surrounded by a single row of columns). About a century later, the more decorative Ionic order developed on the Aegean Islands. Features of this order include volutes (spiral scrolls) on capitals and acroteria (pediment ornaments). The Corinthian order was invented in Athens in the fifth century BC and is typically identified by an acanthus leaf on the capitals. This order was later widely used in ancient Roman architecture.

TEMPLE OF NEPTUNE, PAESTUM, ITALY, c.460 BC

CAPITALS OF THE THREE ORDERS OF ANCIENT GREEK ARCHITECTURE

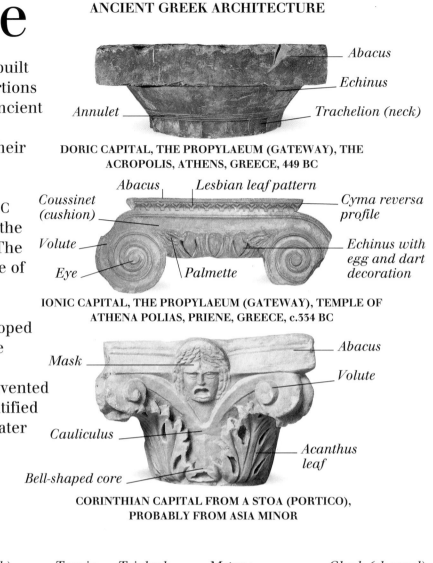

Abacus

Echinus

Annulet

Trachelion (neck)

DORIC CAPITAL, THE PROPYLAEUM (GATEWAY), THE ACROPOLIS, ATHENS, GREECE, 449 BC

Abacus

Lesbian leaf pattern

Coussinet (cushion)

Cyma reversa profile

Volute

Echinus with egg and dart decoration

Eye

Palmette

IONIC CAPITAL, THE PROPYLAEUM (GATEWAY), TEMPLE OF ATHENA POLIAS, PRIENE, GREECE, c.334 BC

Mask

Abacus

Volute

Cauliculus

Acanthus leaf

Bell-shaped core

CORINTHIAN CAPITAL FROM A STOA (PORTICO), PROBABLY FROM ASIA MINOR

Raking cornice

Pediment

Trachelion (neck)

Taenia

Triglyph

Metope

Glyph (channel)

Doric entablature

Pteron (external colonnade)

Euthynteria

Drum

Stylobate

Column of the Doric order

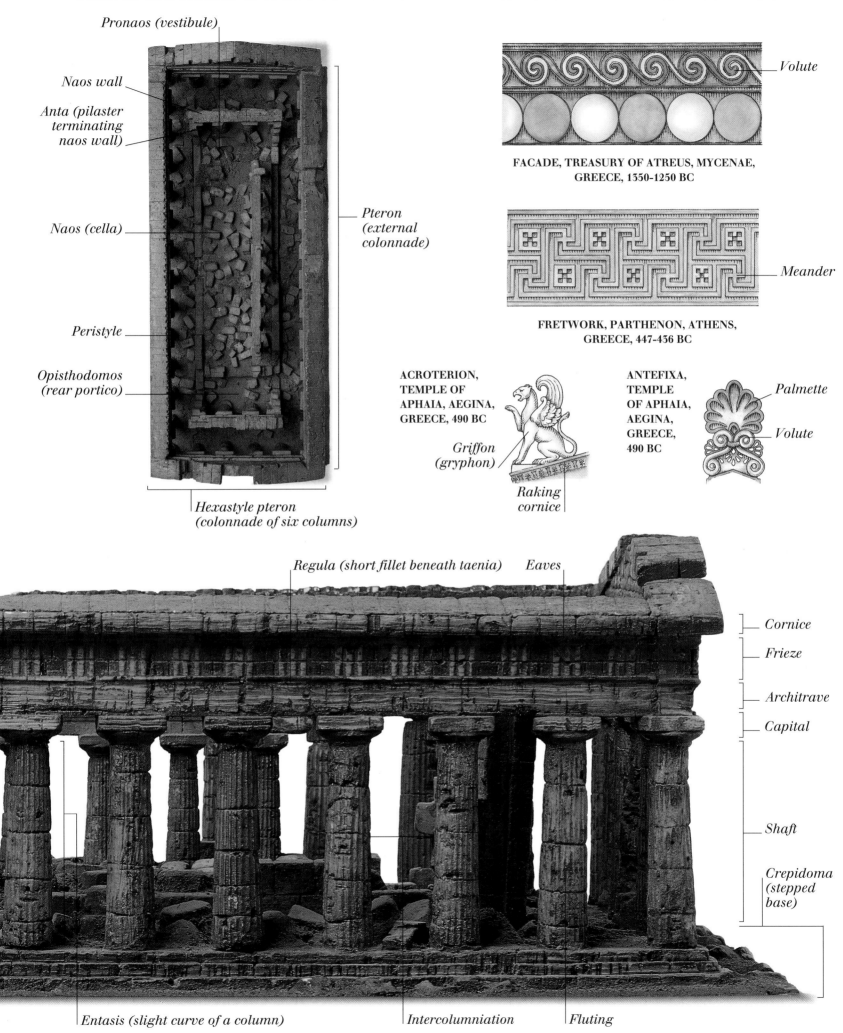

PLAN OF THE TEMPLE OF NEPTUNE, PAESTUM

Pronaos (vestibule)

Naos wall

Anta (pilaster terminating naos wall)

Naos (cella)

Peristyle

Opisthodomos (rear portico)

Pteron (external colonnade)

Hexastyle pteron (colonnade of six columns)

ANCIENT GREEK BUILDING DECORATION

Volute

FACADE, TREASURY OF ATREUS, MYCENAE, GREECE, 1350-1250 BC

Meander

FRETWORK, PARTHENON, ATHENS, GREECE, 447-436 BC

ACROTERION, TEMPLE OF APHAIA, AEGINA, GREECE, 490 BC

Griffon (gryphon)

Raking cornice

ANTEFIXA, TEMPLE OF APHAIA, AEGINA, GREECE, 490 BC

Palmette

Volute

Regula (short fillet beneath taenia)

Eaves

Cornice

Frieze

Architrave

Capital

Shaft

Crepidoma (stepped base)

Entasis (slight curve of a column)

Intercolumniation

Fluting

9

Ancient Rome 1

IN THE EARLY PERIOD OF THE ROMAN EMPIRE extensive use was made of ancient Greek architectural ideas, particularly those of the Corinthian order (see pp. 8-9). As a result, many early Roman buildings—such as the Temple of Vesta (opposite)—closely resemble ancient Greek buildings. A distinctive Roman style began to evolve in the first century AD. This style developed the interiors of buildings (the Greeks had concentrated on the exterior) by wing arches, vaults, and domes inside the buildings and by ornamenting internal walls; many of these features can be seen in the Pantheon. Exterior columns were often used for decorative rather than structural purposes, as in the Colosseum and the Porta Nigra (see pp. 12-13). Smaller buildings had timber frames with wattle-and-daub walls, as in the mill (see pp. 12-13). Roman architecture remained influential for many centuries, with some of its principles being used in the 11th century in Romanesque buildings (see pp. 20-21) and also in the 15th and 16th centuries in Renaissance buildings (see pp. 26-29).

ANCIENT ROMAN BUILDING DECORATION

FESTOON, TEMPLE OF VESTA, TIVOLI, ITALY, c.80 BC

RICHLY DECORATED ROMAN OVUM

INTERIOR OF THE PANTHEON, ROME, ITALY, 118-c.128

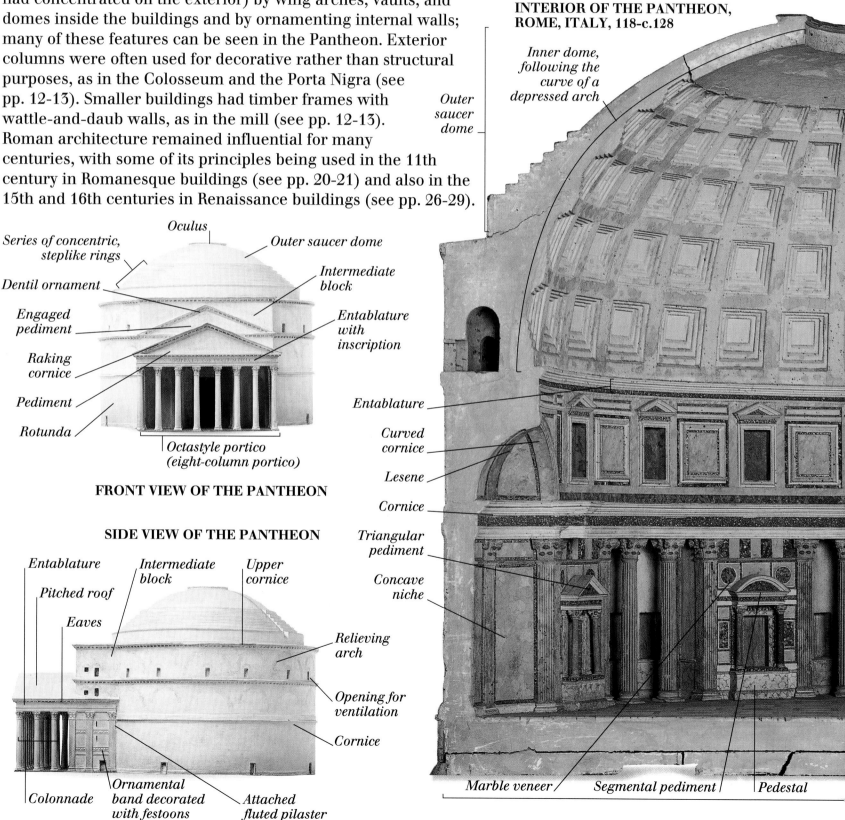

Inner dome, following the curve of a depressed arch

Outer saucer dome

Entablature

Curved cornice

Lesene

Cornice

Triangular pediment

Concave niche

Marble veneer / Segmental pediment / Pedestal

FRONT VIEW OF THE PANTHEON

Oculus

Series of concentric, steplike rings

Outer saucer dome

Dentil ornament

Intermediate block

Engaged pediment

Entablature with inscription

Raking cornice

Pediment

Rotunda

Octastyle portico (eight-column portico)

SIDE VIEW OF THE PANTHEON

Entablature

Intermediate block

Upper cornice

Pitched roof

Eaves

Relieving arch

Opening for ventilation

Cornice

Colonnade

Ornamental band decorated with festoons

Attached fluted pilaster

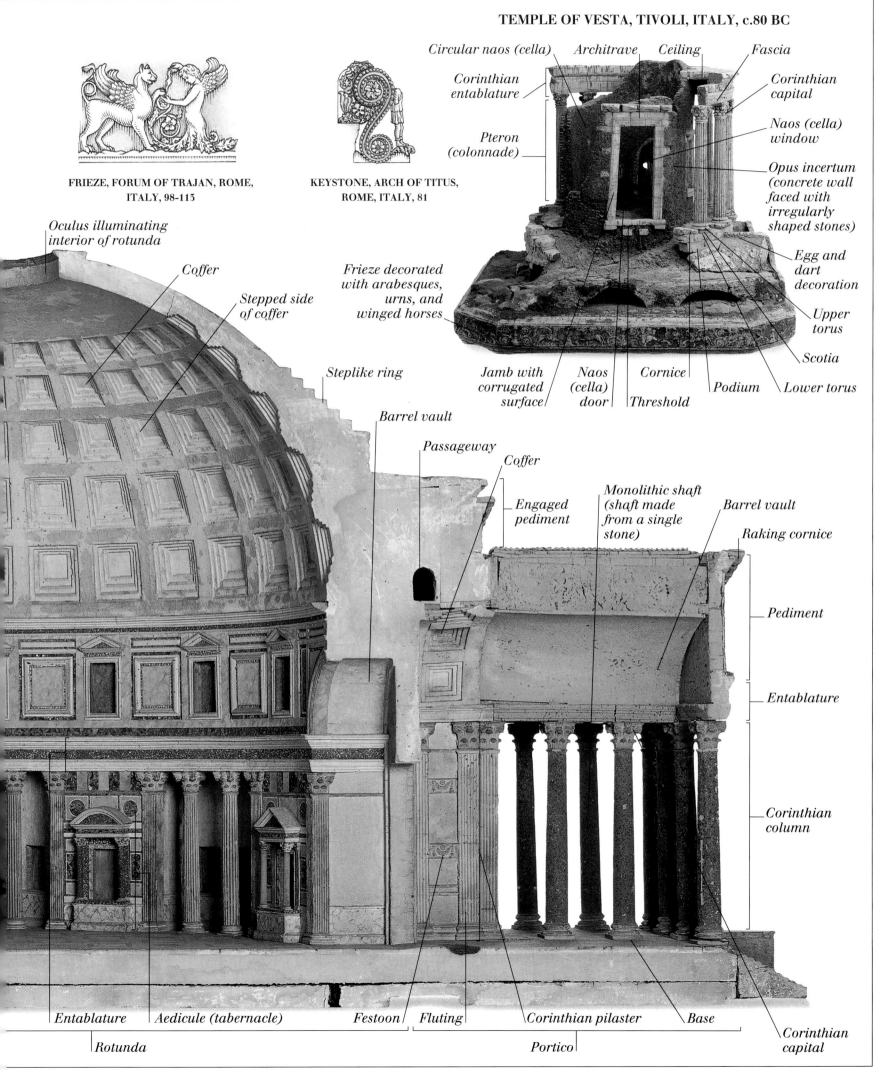

FRIEZE, FORUM OF TRAJAN, ROME, ITALY, 98-113

KEYSTONE, ARCH OF TITUS, ROME, ITALY, 81

TEMPLE OF VESTA, TIVOLI, ITALY, c.80 BC

Circular naos (cella)

Architrave

Ceiling

Fascia

Corinthian entablature

Corinthian capital

Pteron (colonnade)

Naos (cella) window

Opus incertum (concrete wall faced with irregularly shaped stones)

Egg and dart decoration

Upper torus

Scotia

Jamb with corrugated surface

Naos (cella) door

Cornice

Podium

Lower torus

Threshold

Oculus illuminating interior of rotunda

Coffer

Stepped side of coffer

Frieze decorated with arabesques, urns, and winged horses

Steplike ring

Barrel vault

Passageway

Coffer

Monolithic shaft (shaft made from a single stone)

Barrel vault

Raking cornice

Engaged pediment

Pediment

Entablature

Corinthian column

Entablature

Aedicule (tabernacle)

Festoon

Fluting

Corinthian pilaster

Base

Rotunda

Portico

Corinthian capital

Ancient Rome 2

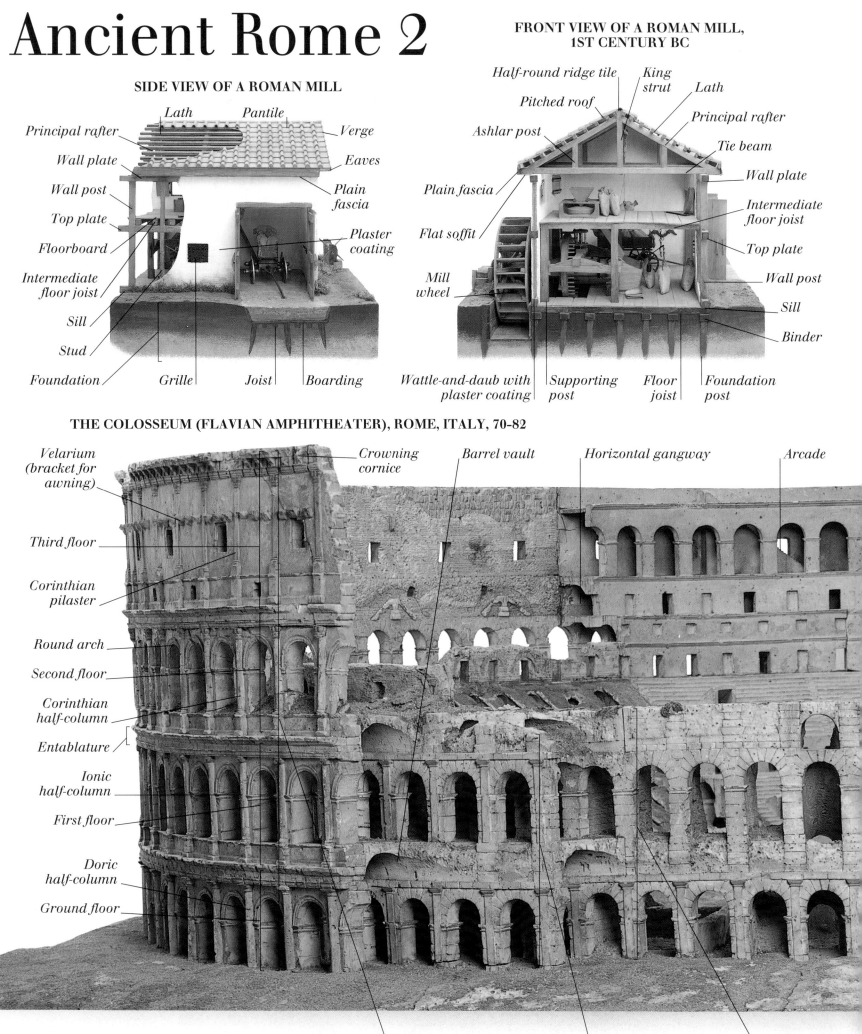

SIDE VIEW OF A ROMAN MILL

Principal rafter

Lath

Pantile

Verge

Wall plate

Eaves

Wall post

Plain fascia

Top plate

Floorboard

Plaster coating

Intermediate floor joist

Sill

Stud

Foundation

Grille

Joist

Boarding

Half-round ridge tile

King strut

Lath

Pitched roof

Ashlar post

Principal rafter

Tie beam

Plain fascia

Wall plate

Flat soffit

Intermediate floor joist

Top plate

Mill wheel

Wall post

Sill

Binder

Wattle-and-daub with plaster coating

Supporting post

Floor joist

Foundation post

THE COLOSSEUM (FLAVIAN AMPHITHEATER), ROME, ITALY, 70-82

Velarium (bracket for awning)

Crowning cornice

Barrel vault

Horizontal gangway

Arcade

Third floor

Corinthian pilaster

Round arch

Second floor

Corinthian half-column

Entablature

Ionic half-column

First floor

Doric half-column

Ground floor

External travertine shell

Intermediate shell

Inner shell

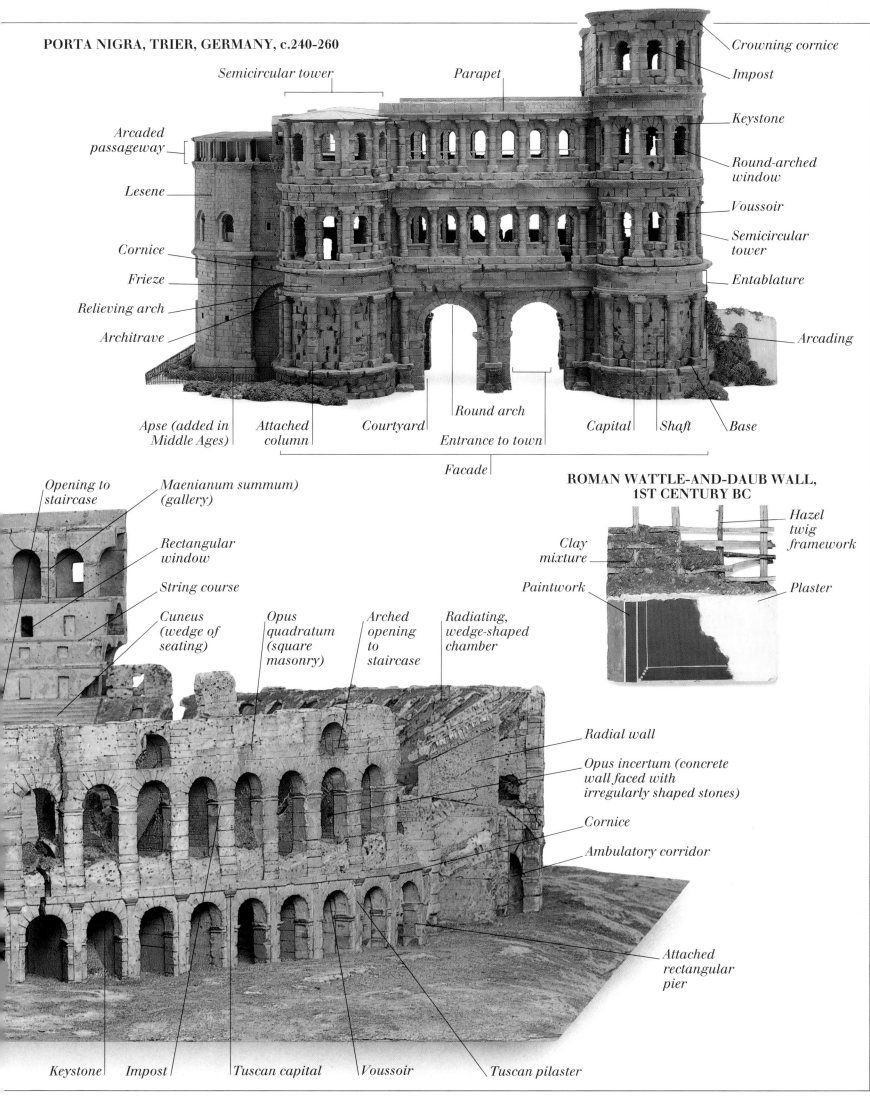

PORTA NIGRA, TRIER, GERMANY, c.240-260

Semicircular tower

Parapet

Crowning cornice

Impost

Arcaded passageway

Keystone

Lesene

Round-arched window

Cornice

Voussoir

Frieze

Semicircular tower

Relieving arch

Entablature

Architrave

Arcading

Apse (added in Middle Ages)

Attached column

Courtyard

Round arch

Entrance to town

Capital

Shaft

Base

Facade

ROMAN WATTLE-AND-DAUB WALL, 1ST CENTURY BC

Opening to staircase

Maenianum summum) (gallery)

Rectangular window

Hazel twig framework

Clay mixture

String course

Paintwork

Plaster

Cuneus (wedge of seating)

Opus quadratum (square masonry)

Arched opening to staircase

Radiating, wedge-shaped chamber

Radial wall

Opus incertum (concrete wall faced with irregularly shaped stones)

Cornice

Ambulatory corridor

Attached rectangular pier

Keystone

Impost

Tuscan capital

Voussoir

Tuscan pilaster

13

Walls

A WALL IS A CONTINUOUS structure that encloses or subdivides a building. The two main types of load-bearing outer wall are frame-construction walls and mass-construction walls. Frame-construction walls have a frame of timber or metal. In timber-framed houses, such as the medieval house below, the open panels between the studs (vertical wall timbers) were filled with wattle (thin wooden laths) and daub (mud or clay). The finished house was often embellished with decorative braces and wooden carvings. A mass-construction wall is a solid structure made of brick or stone.

MEDIEVAL WOODEN WALL ORNAMENT, BRITAIN

Various types of bonding have been developed to increase the strength of brick walls. In English bond, bricks are laid so that alternate courses (layers) on the face of the wall are composed exclusively of either headers (bricks laid widthways) or stretchers (bricks laid lengthways). In Flemish bond, the face of each course consists of alternate headers and stretchers. Stretcher bond is composed of stretchers only. The walls of large buildings were usually built from stone. For example, in St. Paul's Cathedral (opposite), piers (solid masonry supports) bear the weight of huge arches and windows. These piers are decorated with columns and pilasters.

WATTLE AND DAUB

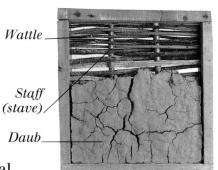

Wattle
Staff (stave)
Daub

BRICKLAYING FORMATIONS

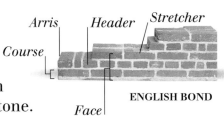

Arris
Header
Stretcher
Course
Face

ENGLISH BOND

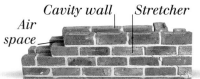

Bed joint
Perpend
Closer
Header
Stretcher

FLEMISH BOND

Cavity wall
Stretcher
Air space

STRETCHER BOND

TYPES OF BRICK

SANDSTONE BRICK

FLINT FACING BRICK

MASS-PRODUCED BRICK, BRITAIN, 19TH CENTURY

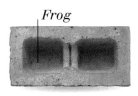

Frog

EARLY METRIC BRICK, BRITAIN, 19TH CENTURY

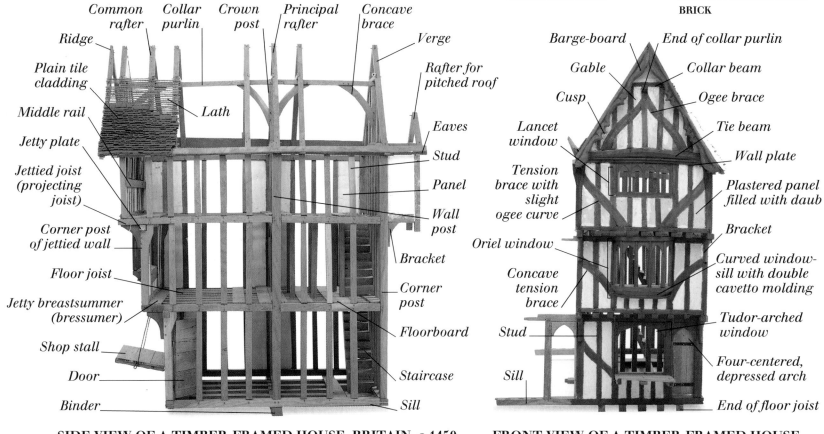

MODERN ENGINEERING BRICK

Common rafter
Collar purlin
Crown post
Principal rafter
Concave brace
Ridge
Verge
Plain tile cladding
Rafter for pitched roof
Middle rail
Lath
Jetty plate
Eaves
Jettied joist (projecting joist)
Stud
Panel
Corner post of jettied wall
Wall post
Floor joist
Bracket
Jetty breastsummer (bressumer)
Corner post
Shop stall
Floorboard
Door
Staircase
Binder
Sill

SIDE VIEW OF A TIMBER-FRAMED HOUSE, BRITAIN, c.1450

Barge-board
End of collar purlin
Gable
Collar beam
Cusp
Ogee brace
Lancet window
Tie beam
Tension brace with slight ogee curve
Wall plate
Plastered panel filled with daub
Oriel window
Bracket
Concave tension brace
Curved window-sill with double cavetto molding
Stud
Tudor-arched window
Sill
Four-centered, depressed arch
End of floor joist

FRONT VIEW OF A TIMBER-FRAMED HOUSE

WOODEN RECONSTRUCTION OF A PIER, ST. PAUL'S CATHEDRAL, LONDON, BRITAIN, 1675-1710 (BY C. WREN)

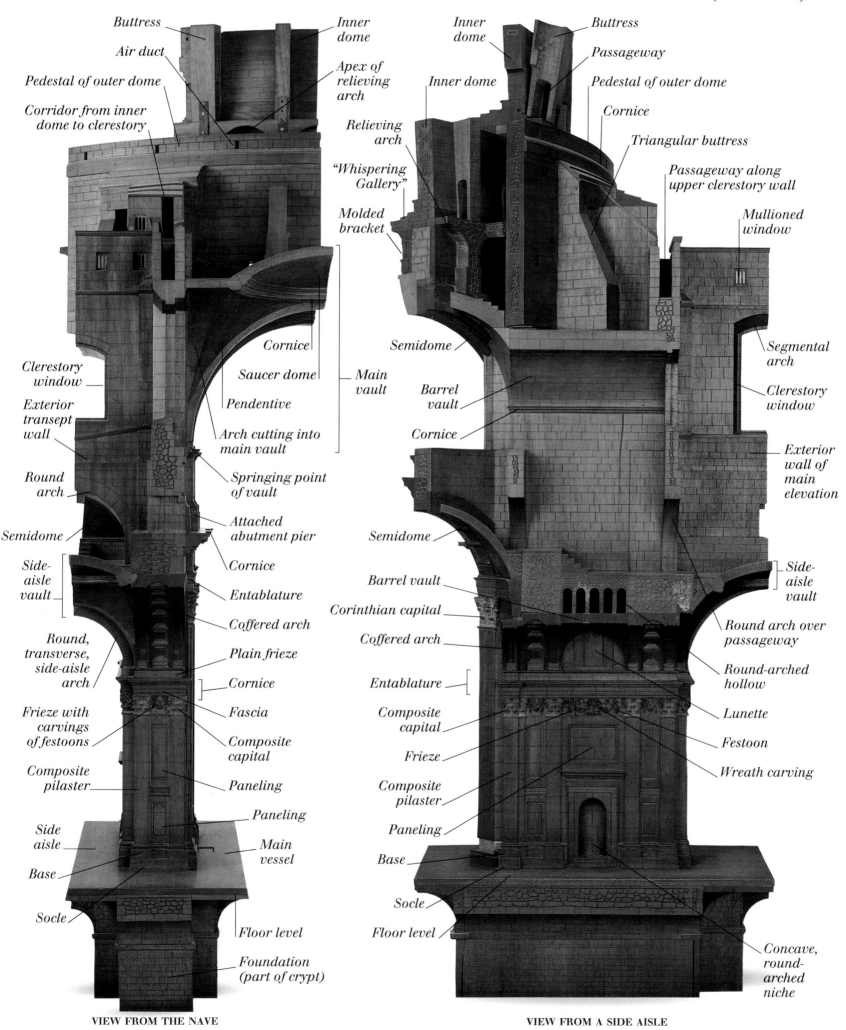

VIEW FROM THE NAVE

Buttress
Air duct
Pedestal of outer dome
Corridor from inner dome to clerestory
Inner dome
Apex of relieving arch
Cornice
Saucer dome
Main vault
Pendentive
Arch cutting into main vault
Clerestory window
Exterior transept wall
Round arch
Semidome
Springing point of vault
Attached abutment pier
Cornice
Entablature
Coffered arch
Side-aisle vault
Plain frieze
Cornice
Fascia
Composite capital
Round, transverse, side-aisle arch
Frieze with carvings of festoons
Composite pilaster
Paneling
Paneling
Side aisle
Main vessel
Base
Socle
Floor level
Foundation (part of crypt)

VIEW FROM A SIDE AISLE

Inner dome
Buttress
Passageway
Inner dome
Pedestal of outer dome
Cornice
Relieving arch
Triangular buttress
"Whispering Gallery"
Molded bracket
Passageway along upper clerestory wall
Mullioned window
Semidome
Segmental arch
Barrel vault
Clerestory window
Cornice
Exterior wall of main elevation
Semidome
Side-aisle vault
Barrel vault
Round arch over passageway
Corinthian capital
Coffered arch
Round-arched hollow
Entablature
Lunette
Composite capital
Festoon
Frieze
Wreath carving
Composite pilaster
Paneling
Base
Socle
Floor level
Concave, round-arched niche

15

Roofs and chimneys

A ROOF HAS TWO BASIC COMPONENTS: a covering and a supporting frame. In pitched (sloping) roofs, the frame consists of inclined rafters and horizontal purlins (timbers) connected to a roof truss by joints such as the mortise and tenon joint or the edge-halfed scarf joint. The most common roof coverings are slates, clay tiles, and asphalt (used to waterproof flat roofs), although thatch and lead are still used, mainly to roof old buildings. A thatched roof consists of layered bundles of straw or reeds attached to the roof with steel or hazel rods and fixed in place by crooks (hooks) driven into the rafters. A chimney consists of a passage (or flue) for the escape of fumes from a fireplace; a chimney stack, which projects above the roof; and a chimney pot on top of the stack. Chimney pots and chimney stacks sometimes have elaborate designs, some of which are shown opposite.

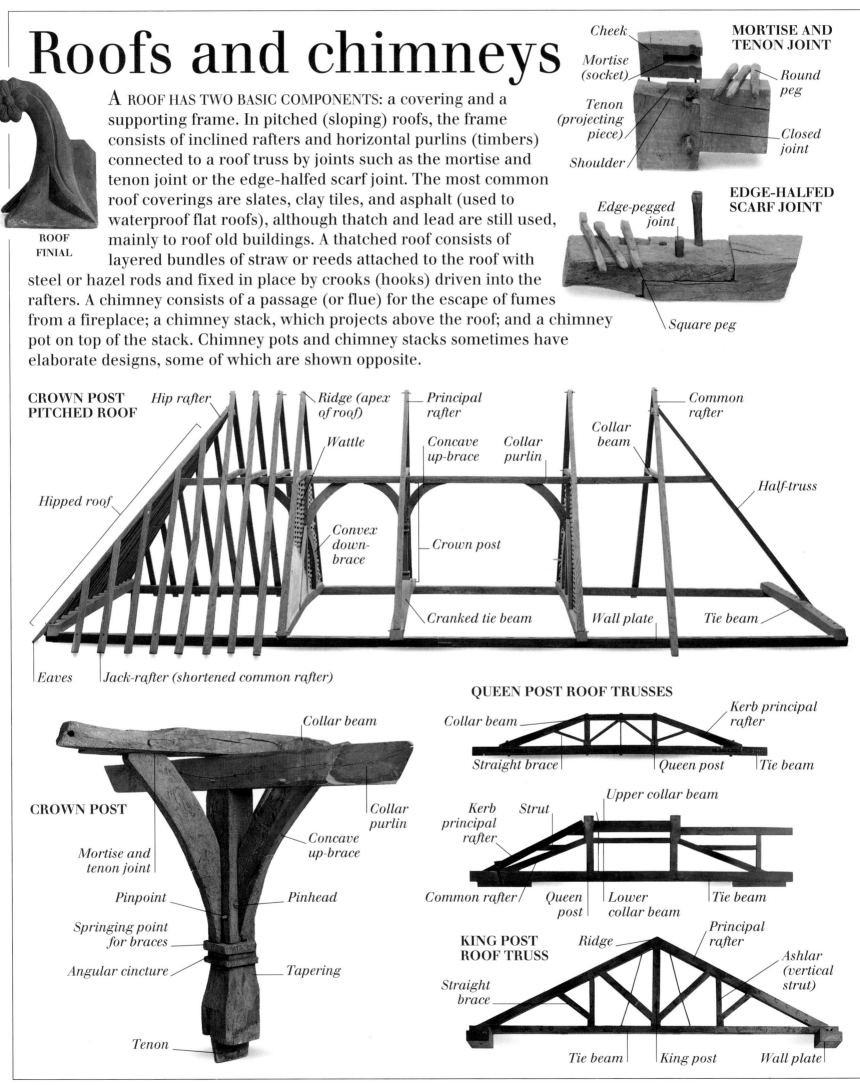

ROOF FINIAL

MORTISE AND TENON JOINT

Cheek
Mortise (socket)
Tenon (projecting piece)
Shoulder
Round peg
Closed joint

EDGE-HALFED SCARF JOINT

Edge-pegged joint
Square peg

CROWN POST PITCHED ROOF

Hip rafter
Ridge (apex of roof)
Principal rafter
Common rafter
Wattle
Concave up-brace
Collar purlin
Collar beam
Half-truss
Hipped roof
Convex down-brace
Crown post
Cranked tie beam
Wall plate
Tie beam
Eaves
Jack-rafter (shortened common rafter)

CROWN POST

Collar beam
Collar purlin
Concave up-brace
Mortise and tenon joint
Pinpoint
Pinhead
Springing point for braces
Angular cincture
Tapering
Tenon

QUEEN POST ROOF TRUSSES

Kerb principal rafter
Collar beam
Straight brace
Queen post
Tie beam
Upper collar beam
Kerb principal rafter
Strut
Common rafter
Queen post
Lower collar beam
Tie beam

KING POST ROOF TRUSS

Ridge
Principal rafter
Ashlar (vertical strut)
Straight brace
Tie beam
King post
Wall plate

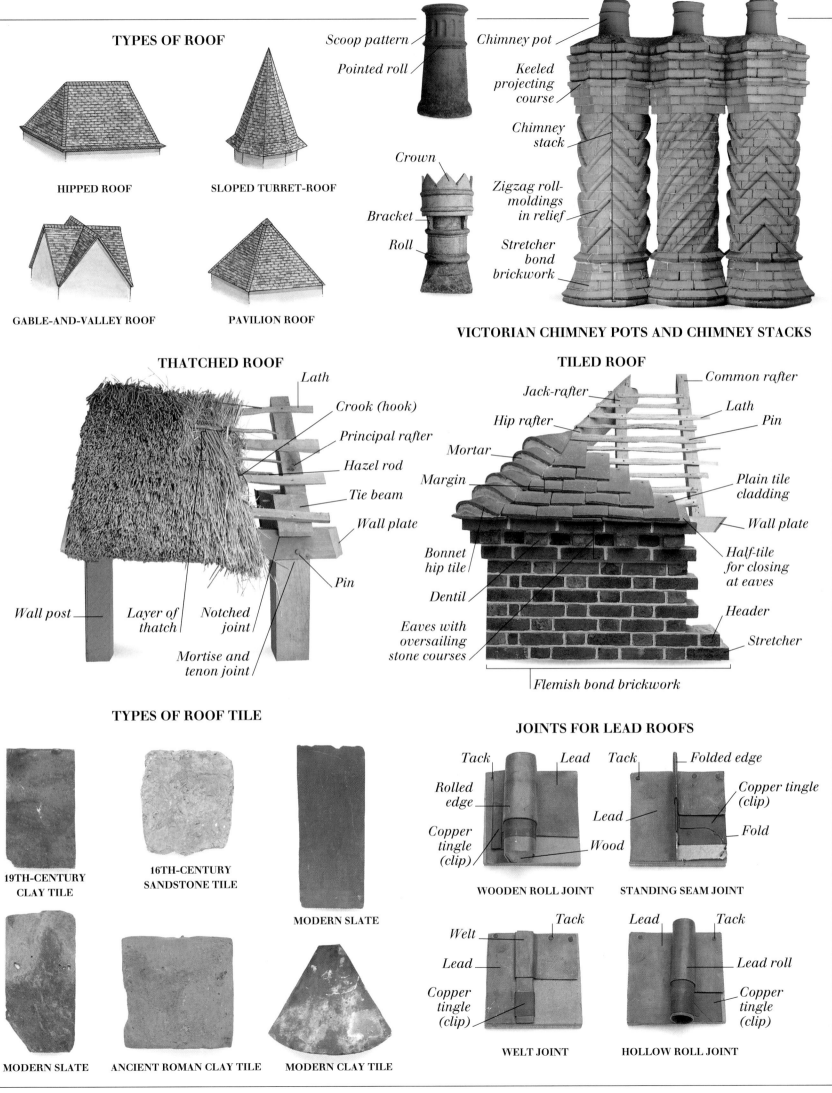

TYPES OF ROOF

HIPPED ROOF

SLOPED TURRET-ROOF

GABLE-AND-VALLEY ROOF

PAVILION ROOF

Scoop pattern

Pointed roll

Chimney pot

Keeled projecting course

Chimney stack

Crown

Bracket

Roll

Zigzag roll-moldings in relief

Stretcher bond brickwork

VICTORIAN CHIMNEY POTS AND CHIMNEY STACKS

THATCHED ROOF

Lath

Crook (hook)

Principal rafter

Hazel rod

Tie beam

Wall plate

Pin

Wall post

Layer of thatch

Notched joint

Mortise and tenon joint

TILED ROOF

Jack-rafter

Hip rafter

Mortar

Margin

Common rafter

Lath

Pin

Plain tile cladding

Wall plate

Half-tile for closing at eaves

Bonnet hip tile

Dentil

Eaves with oversailing stone courses

Header

Stretcher

Flemish bond brickwork

TYPES OF ROOF TILE

19TH-CENTURY CLAY TILE

16TH-CENTURY SANDSTONE TILE

MODERN SLATE

MODERN SLATE

ANCIENT ROMAN CLAY TILE

MODERN CLAY TILE

JOINTS FOR LEAD ROOFS

Tack

Lead

Rolled edge

Copper tingle (clip)

Wood

Tack

Folded edge

Copper tingle (clip)

Lead

Fold

WOODEN ROLL JOINT

STANDING SEAM JOINT

Welt

Lead

Copper tingle (clip)

Tack

Lead

Tack

Lead roll

Copper tingle (clip)

WELT JOINT

HOLLOW ROLL JOINT

Medieval castles and houses

WARFARE WAS COMMON IN EUROPE in the Middle Ages, and many monarchs and nobles built castles as a form of defense. Typical medieval castles have outer walls surrounding a moat. Inside the moat is a bailey (courtyard), protected by a chemise (jacket wall). The innermost and strongest part of a medieval castle is the keep. There are two main types of keep: towers called donjons, such as the Tour de César and Coucy-le-Château in France, and rectangular keeps ("hall-keeps"), such as the Tower of London. Castles were often guarded by salients (projecting fortifications), like those of the Bastille. Medieval houses typically had timber cruck (tent-like) frames, wattle-and-daub walls (see pp. 14-15), and pitched roofs, like those on medieval London Bridge (opposite).

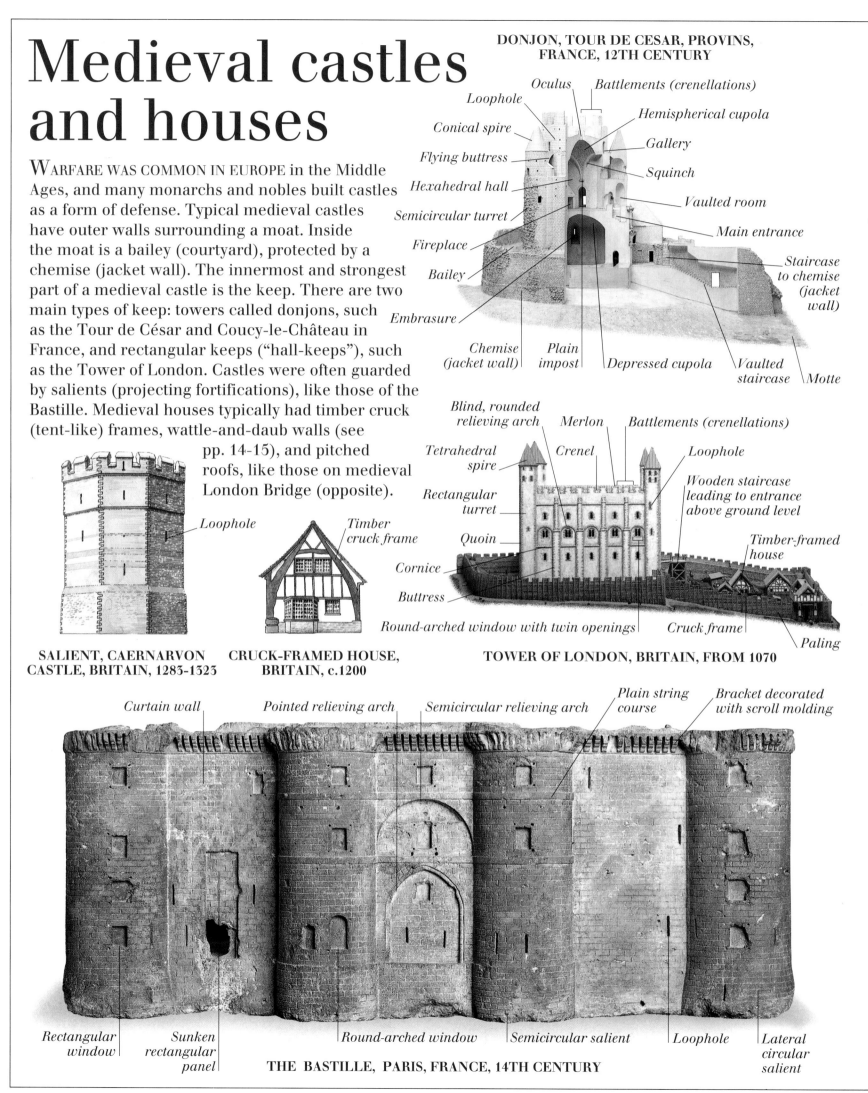

DONJON, TOUR DE CESAR, PROVINS, FRANCE, 12TH CENTURY

Oculus
Loophole
Battlements (crenellations)
Conical spire
Hemispherical cupola
Flying buttress
Gallery
Hexahedral hall
Squinch
Semicircular turret
Vaulted room
Fireplace
Main entrance
Bailey
Staircase to chemise (jacket wall)
Embrasure
Chemise (jacket wall)
Plain impost
Depressed cupola
Vaulted staircase
Motte

Loophole

SALIENT, CAERNARVON CASTLE, BRITAIN, 1283-1323

Timber cruck frame

CRUCK-FRAMED HOUSE, BRITAIN, c.1200

Blind, rounded relieving arch
Merlon
Battlements (crenellations)
Tetrahedral spire
Crenel
Loophole
Rectangular turret
Wooden staircase leading to entrance above ground level
Quoin
Timber-framed house
Cornice
Buttress
Round-arched window with twin openings
Cruck frame
Paling

TOWER OF LONDON, BRITAIN, FROM 1070

Curtain wall
Pointed relieving arch
Semicircular relieving arch
Plain string course
Bracket decorated with scroll molding

Rectangular window
Sunken rectangular panel
Round-arched window
Semicircular salient
Loophole
Lateral circular salient

THE BASTILLE, PARIS, FRANCE, 14TH CENTURY

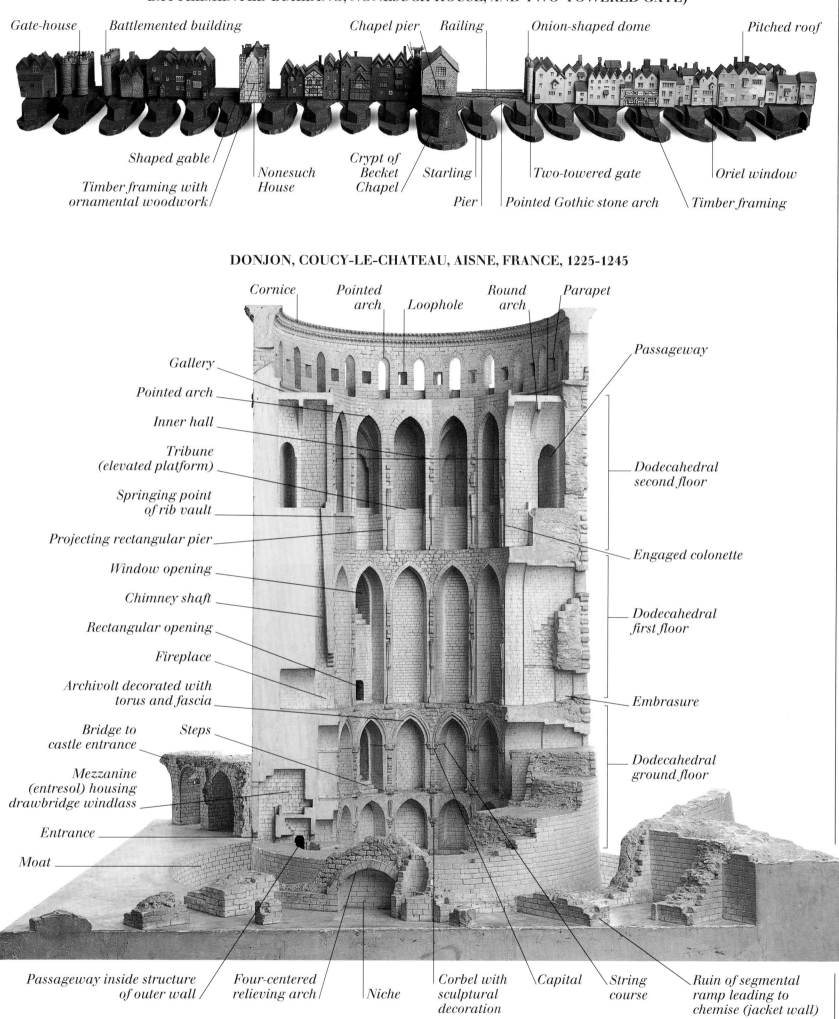

MEDIEVAL LONDON BRIDGE, BRITAIN, 1176 (WITH 14TH-CENTURY BATTLEMENTED BUILDING, NONESUCH HOUSE, AND TWO-TOWERED GATE)

Gate-house

Battlemented building

Chapel pier

Railing

Onion-shaped dome

Pitched roof

Shaped gable

Nonesuch House

Crypt of Becket Chapel

Starling

Two-towered gate

Oriel window

Timber framing with ornamental woodwork

Pier

Pointed Gothic stone arch

Timber framing

DONJON, COUCY-LE-CHATEAU, AISNE, FRANCE, 1225-1245

Cornice

Pointed arch

Loophole

Round arch

Parapet

Gallery

Passageway

Pointed arch

Inner hall

Tribune (elevated platform)

Dodecahedral second floor

Springing point of rib vault

Projecting rectangular pier

Engaged colonette

Window opening

Chimney shaft

Dodecahedral first floor

Rectangular opening

Fireplace

Archivolt decorated with torus and fascia

Embrasure

Bridge to castle entrance

Steps

Mezzanine (entresol) housing drawbridge windlass

Dodecahedral ground floor

Entrance

Moat

Passageway inside structure of outer wall

Four-centered relieving arch

Niche

Corbel with sculptural decoration

Capital

String course

Ruin of segmental ramp leading to chemise (jacket wall)

Medieval churches

LARGE NUMBERS OF CHURCHES were built in Europe in the Middle Ages. European churches of this period typically have high vaults supported by massive piers and columns. In the 10th century, the Romanesque style developed. Romanesque architects adopted many Roman or early Christian architectural ideas, such as cross-shaped ground plans—like that of Angoulême Cathedral (opposite)—and the basilican system of a nave with a central vessel and side aisles. In the mid-12th century, flying buttresses and pointed vaults appeared. These features later became widely used in Gothic architecture (see pp. 22-23). Bagneux Church (opposite) has both styles: a Romanesque tower and a Gothic nave and choir.

CHURCH ROOF BOSS, BRITAIN

ROMANESQUE CAPITALS

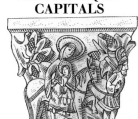

"THE FLIGHT INTO EGYPT" CAPITAL, CATHEDRAL OF ST. LAZARE, AUTUN, FRANCE, 1120-1130

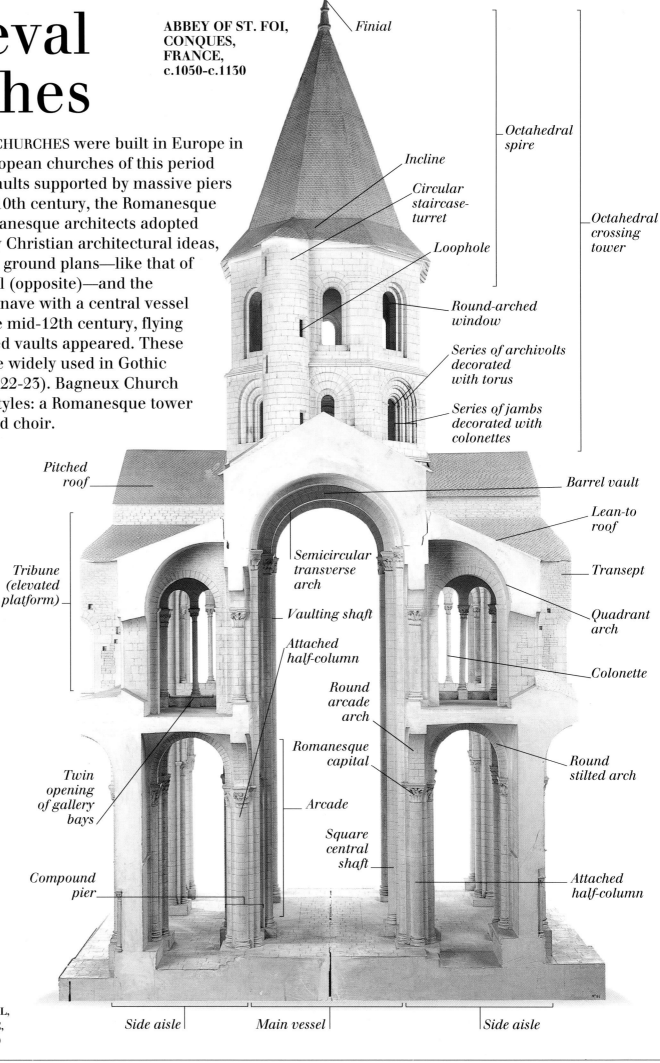

Finial

Incline

Circular staircase-turret

Loophole

Octahedral spire

Octahedral crossing tower

Round-arched window

Series of archivolts decorated with torus

Series of jambs decorated with colonettes

Pitched roof

Barrel vault

Lean-to roof

Tribune (elevated platform)

Semicircular transverse arch

Transept

Vaulting shaft

Quadrant arch

Attached half-column

Colonette

Round arcade arch

Romanesque capital

Round stilted arch

Twin opening of gallery bays

Arcade

Compound pier

Square central shaft

Attached half-column

Side aisle

Main vessel

Side aisle

"CHRIST IN MAJESTY" CAPITAL, BASILICA OF ST. MADELEINE, VEZELAY, FRANCE, 1120-1140

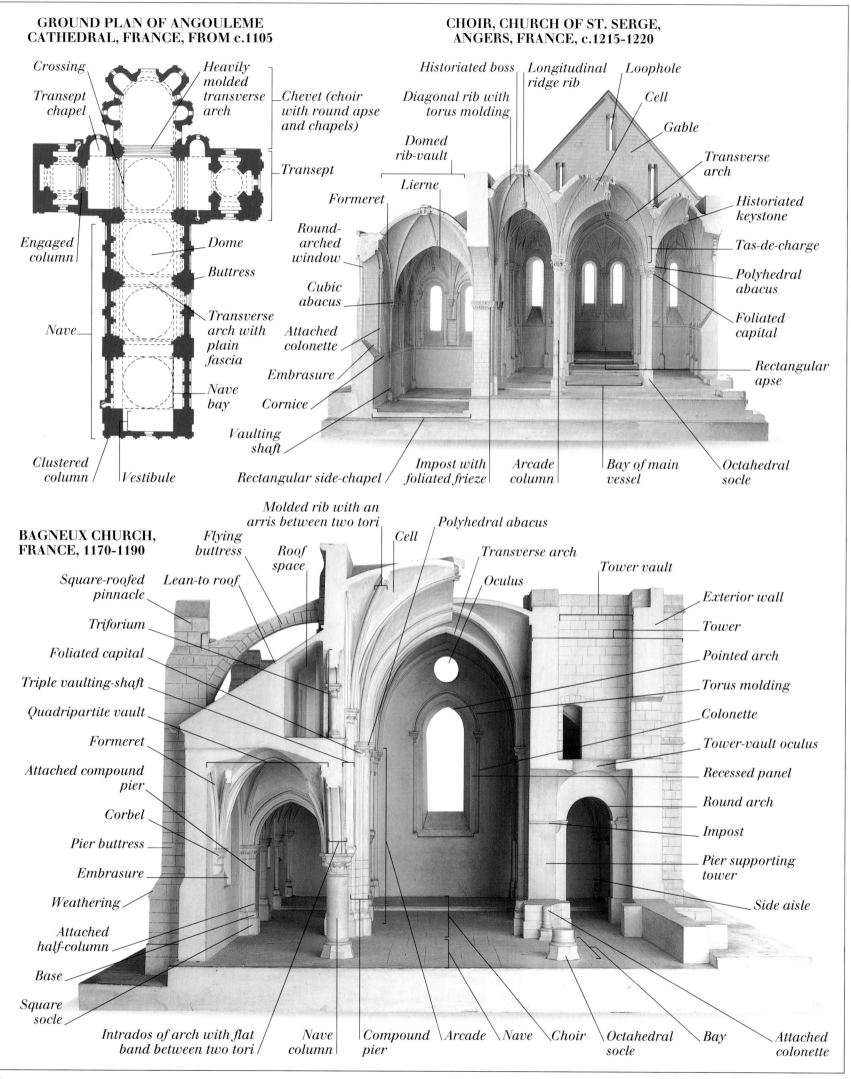

GROUND PLAN OF ANGOULEME CATHEDRAL, FRANCE, FROM c.1105

Crossing

Transept chapel

Heavily molded transverse arch

Chevet (choir with round apse and chapels)

Transept

Engaged column

Dome

Buttress

Nave

Transverse arch with plain fascia

Nave bay

Clustered column

Vestibule

CHOIR, CHURCH OF ST. SERGE, ANGERS, FRANCE, c.1215-1220

Historiated boss

Longitudinal ridge rib

Loophole

Diagonal rib with torus molding

Cell

Gable

Domed rib-vault

Transverse arch

Lierne

Formeret

Historiated keystone

Round-arched window

Tas-de-charge

Cubic abacus

Polyhedral abacus

Attached colonette

Foliated capital

Embrasure

Rectangular apse

Cornice

Vaulting shaft

Rectangular side-chapel

Impost with foliated frieze

Arcade column

Bay of main vessel

Octahedral socle

BAGNEUX CHURCH, FRANCE, 1170-1190

Molded rib with an arris between two tori

Flying buttress

Roof space

Cell

Polyhedral abacus

Transverse arch

Oculus

Tower vault

Square-roofed pinnacle

Lean-to roof

Exterior wall

Triforium

Tower

Foliated capital

Pointed arch

Triple vaulting-shaft

Torus molding

Quadripartite vault

Colonette

Formeret

Tower-vault oculus

Attached compound pier

Recessed panel

Corbel

Round arch

Pier buttress

Impost

Embrasure

Pier supporting tower

Weathering

Side aisle

Attached half-column

Base

Square socle

Intrados of arch with flat band between two tori

Nave column

Compound pier

Arcade

Nave

Choir

Octahedral socle

Bay

Attached colonette

Gothic 1

GOTHIC BUILDINGS are characterized by rib vaults, pointed or lancet arches, flying buttresses, decorative tracery and gables, and stained-glass windows. Typical Gothic buildings include the Cathedrals of Salisbury and old St. Paul's in England, and Notre Dame de Paris in France (see pp. 24-25). The Gothic style developed out of Romanesque architecture in France (see pp. 20-21) in the mid-12th century and then spread throughout Europe. The decorative elements of Gothic architecture became highly developed in buildings of the English Decorated style (late 13th-14th century) and the French Flamboyant style (15th-16th century). These styles are exemplified by the tower of Salisbury Cathedral and by the staircase in the Church of St. Maclou (see pp. 24-25), respectively. In both of these styles, embellishments such as ballflowers and curvilinear (flowing) tracery were used liberally. The English Perpendicular style (late 14th-15th century), which followed the Decorated style, emphasized the vertical and horizontal elements of a building. A notable feature of this style is the hammer-beam roof.

GOTHIC STAINED GLASS WITH FOLIATED SCROLL MOTIF, ON WOODEN FORM

GROUND PLAN OF SALISBURY CATHEDRAL

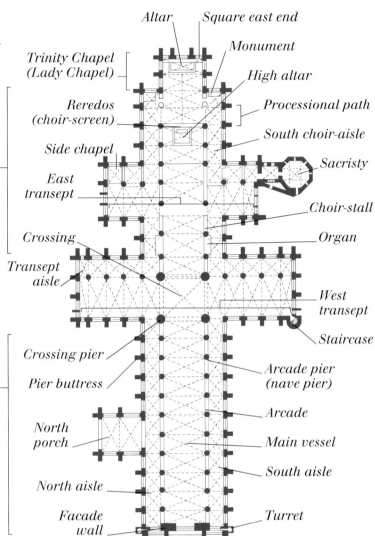

- Altar
- Square east end
- Monument
- Trinity Chapel (Lady Chapel)
- High altar
- Reredos (choir-screen)
- Processional path
- Side chapel
- South choir-aisle
- Choir
- Sacristy
- East transept
- Choir-stall
- Crossing
- Organ
- Transept aisle
- West transept
- Crossing pier
- Staircase
- Pier buttress
- Arcade pier (nave pier)
- Arcade
- Nave
- North porch
- Main vessel
- South aisle
- North aisle
- Facade wall
- Turret

GOTHIC TORUS WITH BALLFLOWERS

- Limestone block
- Block members carved into rolls
- Block members cut polygonally
- Pencil guideline
- Early stage of ballflower carving

BLOCK AFTER INITIAL CUTTING

BLOCK WITH MEMBERS CUT INTO ROLLS

- Torus
- Ballflower
- Fillet
- Mason's mark

FINISHED BLOCK

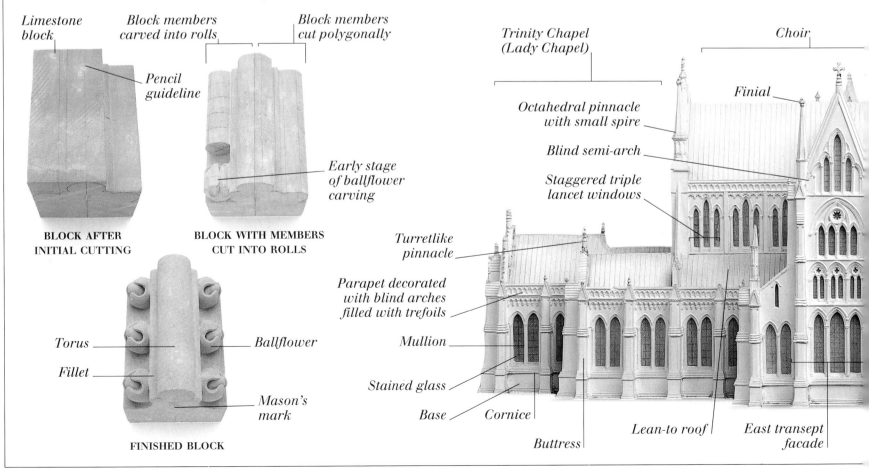

- Trinity Chapel (Lady Chapel)
- Choir
- Finial
- Octahedral pinnacle with small spire
- Blind semi-arch
- Staggered triple lancet windows
- Turretlike pinnacle
- Parapet decorated with blind arches filled with trefoils
- Mullion
- Stained glass
- Base
- Cornice
- Lean-to roof
- East transept facade
- Buttress

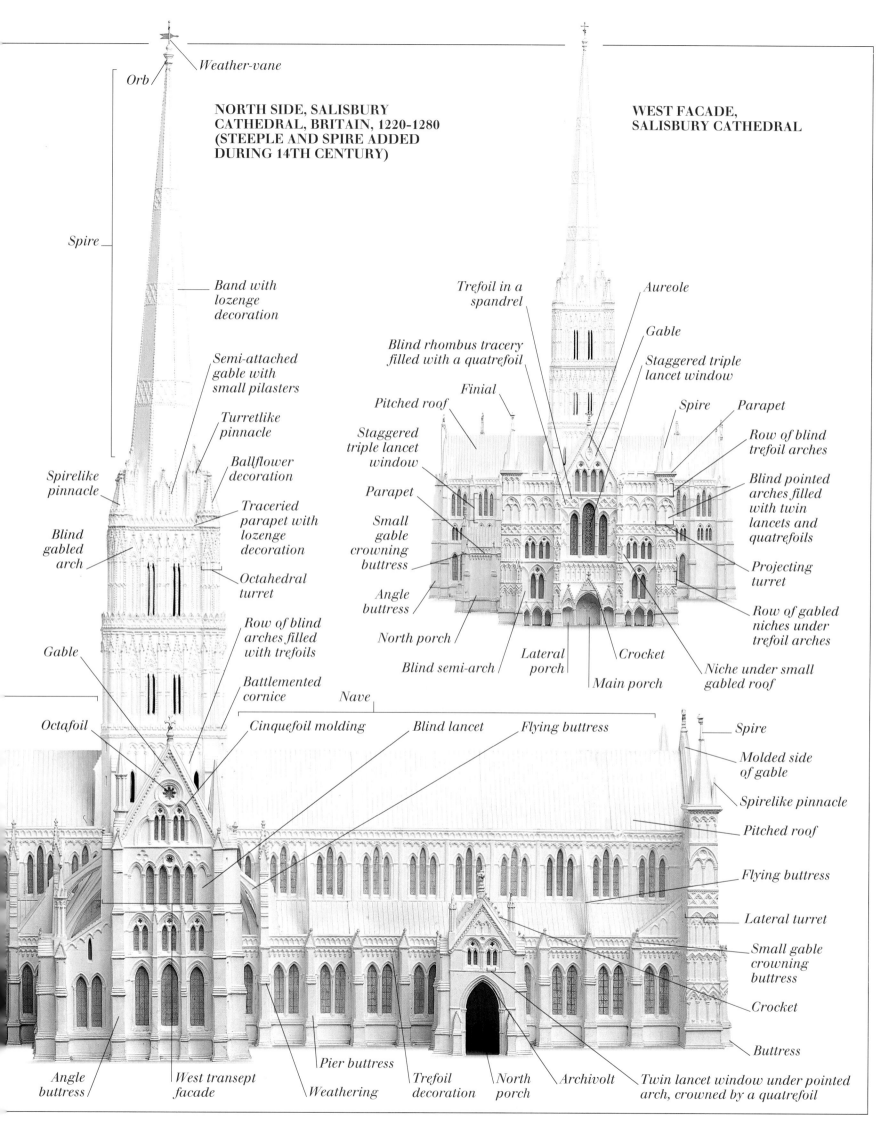

NORTH SIDE, SALISBURY
CATHEDRAL, BRITAIN, 1220-1280
(STEEPLE AND SPIRE ADDED
DURING 14TH CENTURY)

WEST FACADE,
SALISBURY CATHEDRAL

Orb

Weather-vane

Spire

Band with
lozenge
decoration

Semi-attached
gable with
small pilasters

Turretlike
pinnacle

Spirelike
pinnacle

Ballflower
decoration

Blind
gabled
arch

Traceried
parapet with
lozenge
decoration

Octahedral
turret

Gable

Row of blind
arches filled
with trefoils

Octafoil

Battlemented
cornice

Nave

Cinquefoil molding

Blind lancet

Flying buttress

Trefoil in a
spandrel

Aureole

Gable

Blind rhombus tracery
filled with a quatrefoil

Staggered triple
lancet window

Finial

Pitched roof

Spire

Parapet

Staggered
triple lancet
window

Row of blind
trefoil arches

Parapet

Blind pointed
arches filled
with twin
lancets and
quatrefoils

Small
gable
crowning
buttress

Angle
buttress

Projecting
turret

North porch

Row of gabled
niches under
trefoil arches

Blind semi-arch

Lateral
porch

Crocket

Niche under small
gabled roof

Main porch

Spire

Molded side
of gable

Spirelike pinnacle

Pitched roof

Flying buttress

Lateral turret

Small gable
crowning
buttress

Crocket

Angle
buttress

West transept
facade

Pier buttress

Weathering

Trefoil
decoration

North
porch

Archivolt

Buttress

Twin lancet window under pointed
arch, crowned by a quatrefoil

23

Gothic 2

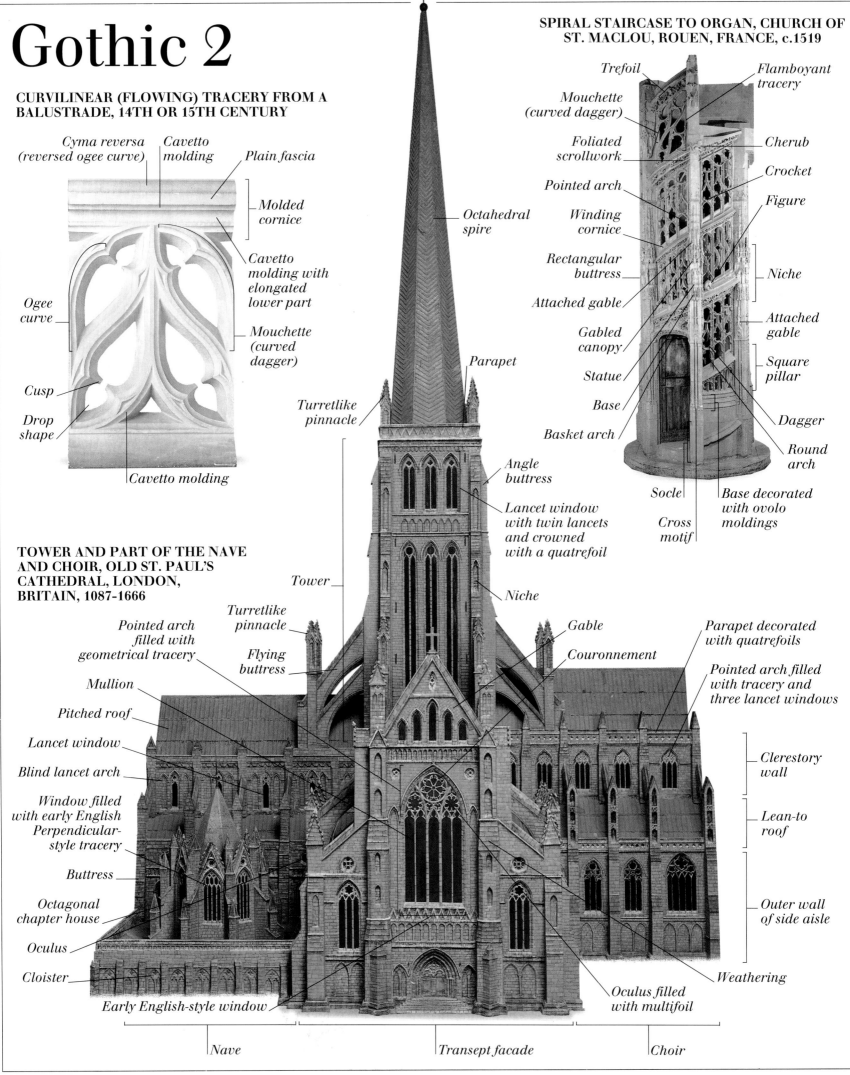

CURVILINEAR (FLOWING) TRACERY FROM A BALUSTRADE, 14TH OR 15TH CENTURY

Cyma reversa (reversed ogee curve)

Cavetto molding

Plain fascia

Molded cornice

Cavetto molding with elongated lower part

Ogee curve

Mouchette (curved dagger)

Cusp

Drop shape

Cavetto molding

SPIRAL STAIRCASE TO ORGAN, CHURCH OF ST. MACLOU, ROUEN, FRANCE, c.1519

Trefoil

Mouchette (curved dagger)

Flamboyant tracery

Foliated scrollwork

Cherub

Pointed arch

Crocket

Winding cornice

Figure

Rectangular buttress

Niche

Attached gable

Gabled canopy

Attached gable

Statue

Square pillar

Base

Basket arch

Dagger

Round arch

Socle

Cross motif

Base decorated with ovolo moldings

TOWER AND PART OF THE NAVE AND CHOIR, OLD ST. PAUL'S CATHEDRAL, LONDON, BRITAIN, 1087–1666

Octahedral spire

Parapet

Turretlike pinnacle

Angle buttress

Lancet window with twin lancets and crowned with a quatrefoil

Tower

Niche

Pointed arch filled with geometrical tracery

Turretlike pinnacle

Gable

Couronnement

Parapet decorated with quatrefoils

Flying buttress

Pointed arch filled with tracery and three lancet windows

Mullion

Pitched roof

Lancet window

Blind lancet arch

Clerestory wall

Window filled with early English Perpendicular-style tracery

Lean-to roof

Buttress

Octagonal chapter house

Oculus

Outer wall of side aisle

Cloister

Weathering

Early English-style window

Oculus filled with multifoil

Nave

Transept facade

Choir

24

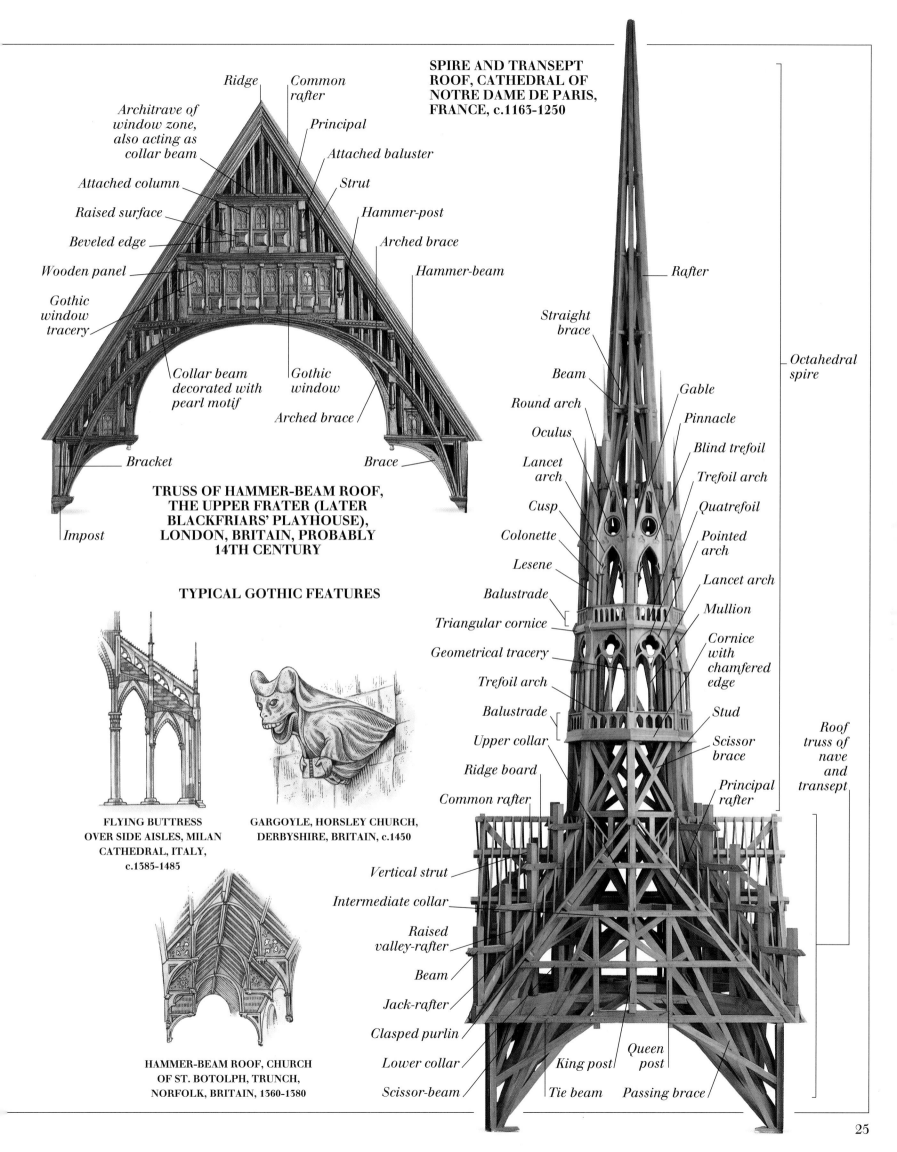

Ridge

Common rafter

Architrave of window zone, also acting as collar beam

Principal

Attached baluster

Attached column

Strut

Raised surface

Hammer-post

Beveled edge

Arched brace

Wooden panel

Hammer-beam

Gothic window tracery

Collar beam decorated with pearl motif

Gothic window

Arched brace

Bracket

Brace

Impost

TRUSS OF HAMMER-BEAM ROOF, THE UPPER FRATER (LATER BLACKFRIARS' PLAYHOUSE), LONDON, BRITAIN, PROBABLY 14TH CENTURY

SPIRE AND TRANSEPT ROOF, CATHEDRAL OF NOTRE DAME DE PARIS, FRANCE, c.1163-1250

TYPICAL GOTHIC FEATURES

FLYING BUTTRESS OVER SIDE AISLES, MILAN CATHEDRAL, ITALY, c.1385-1485

GARGOYLE, HORSLEY CHURCH, DERBYSHIRE, BRITAIN, c.1450

HAMMER-BEAM ROOF, CHURCH OF ST. BOTOLPH, TRUNCH, NORFOLK, BRITAIN, 1360-1380

Rafter

Straight brace

Octahedral spire

Beam

Gable

Round arch

Pinnacle

Oculus

Blind trefoil

Lancet arch

Trefoil arch

Cusp

Quatrefoil

Colonette

Pointed arch

Lesene

Lancet arch

Balustrade

Mullion

Triangular cornice

Cornice with chamfered edge

Geometrical tracery

Trefoil arch

Balustrade

Stud

Upper collar

Scissor brace

Ridge board

Principal rafter

Common rafter

Roof truss of nave and transept

Vertical strut

Intermediate collar

Raised valley-rafter

Beam

Jack-rafter

Clasped purlin

Queen post

Lower collar

King post

Scissor-beam

Tie beam

Passing brace

Renaissance 1

THE RENAISSANCE was a period in European history—lasting roughly from the 14th century to the mid-17th century—during which the arts and sciences underwent great changes. In architecture, these changes were marked by a return to the classical forms and proportions of ancient Roman buildings. The Renaissance originated in Italy, and the buildings most characteristic of its style can be found there, such as the Palazzo Strozzi shown here. Mannerism is a branch of the Renaissance style that distorts the classical forms; an example is the Laurentian Library staircase. As the Renaissance style spread to other European countries, many of its features were incorporated into the local architecture. For example, the Château de Montal in France (see pp. 28-29) incorporates aedicules (tabernacles).

FACADE ON TO PIAZZA, PALAZZO STROZZI

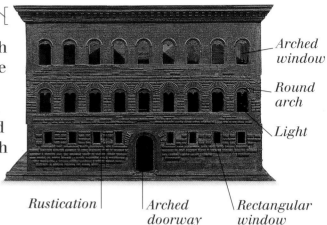

Crowning cornice

Arched window

Round arch

Light

Rustication

Arched doorway

Rectangular window

SIDE VIEW OF PALAZZO STROZZI, FLORENCE, ITALY, 1489 (BY G. DA SANGALLO, B. DA MAIANO, AND CRONACA)

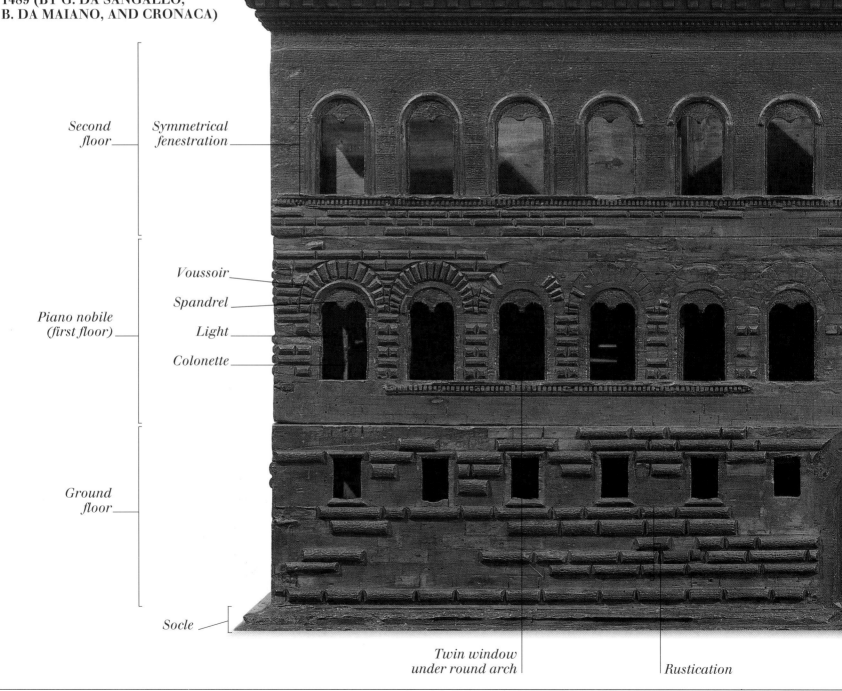

Second floor

Symmetrical fenestration

Piano nobile (first floor)

Voussoir

Spandrel

Light

Colonette

Ground floor

Socle

Twin window under round arch

Rustication

DETAILS FROM ITALIAN RENAISSANCE BUILDINGS

**PANEL FROM DRUM OF DOME,
FLORENCE CATHEDRAL, 1420-1436**

**COFFERING IN DOME,
PAZZI CHAPEL,
FLORENCE, 1429-1461**

**STAIRCASE,
LAURENTIAN LIBRARY,
FLORENCE, 1559**

**PORTICO, VILLA ROTUNDA,
VICENZA, 1567-1569**

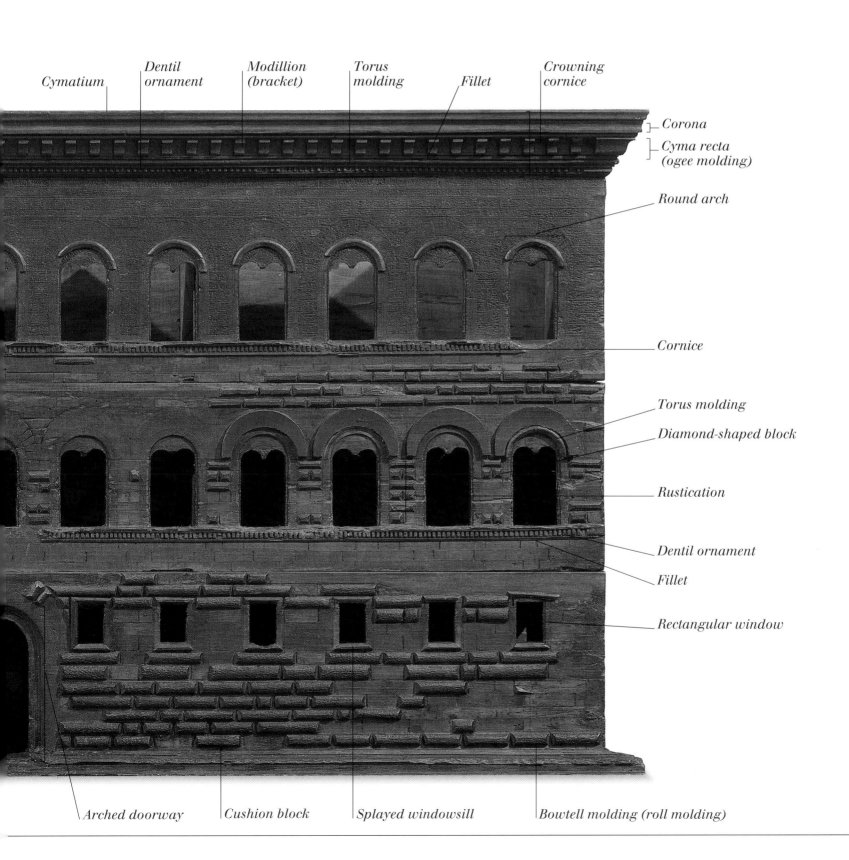

Cymatium

Dentil ornament

Modillion (bracket)

Torus molding

Fillet

Crowning cornice

Corona

Cyma recta (ogee molding)

Round arch

Cornice

Torus molding

Diamond-shaped block

Rustication

Dentil ornament

Fillet

Rectangular window

Arched doorway

Cushion block

Splayed windowsill

Bowtell molding (roll molding)

Renaissance 2

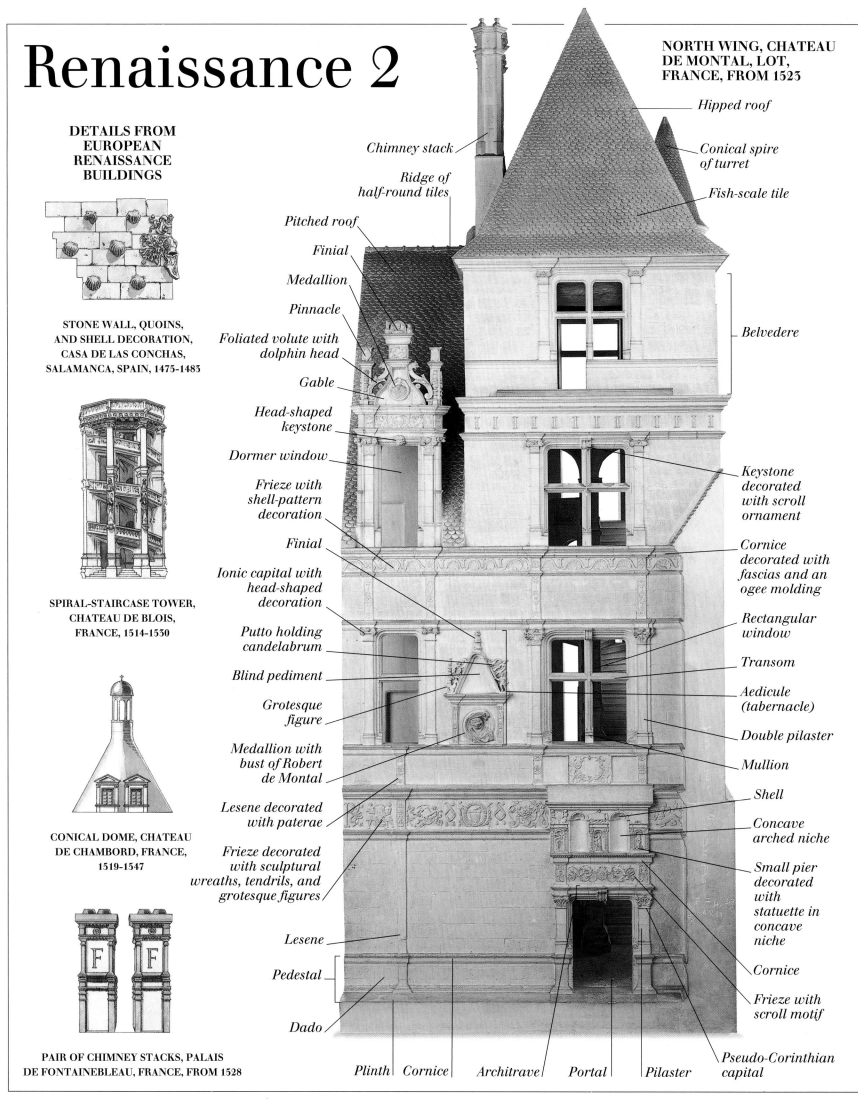

DETAILS FROM EUROPEAN RENAISSANCE BUILDINGS

STONE WALL, QUOINS, AND SHELL DECORATION, CASA DE LAS CONCHAS, SALAMANCA, SPAIN, 1475-1483

SPIRAL-STAIRCASE TOWER, CHATEAU DE BLOIS, FRANCE, 1514-1530

CONICAL DOME, CHATEAU DE CHAMBORD, FRANCE, 1519-1547

PAIR OF CHIMNEY STACKS, PALAIS DE FONTAINEBLEAU, FRANCE, FROM 1528

NORTH WING, CHATEAU DE MONTAL, LOT, FRANCE, FROM 1523

Hipped roof

Conical spire of turret

Fish-scale tile

Belvedere

Keystone decorated with scroll ornament

Cornice decorated with fascias and an ogee molding

Rectangular window

Transom

Aedicule (tabernacle)

Double pilaster

Mullion

Shell

Concave arched niche

Small pier decorated with statuette in concave niche

Cornice

Frieze with scroll motif

Pseudo-Corinthian capital

Chimney stack

Ridge of half-round tiles

Pitched roof

Finial

Medallion

Pinnacle

Foliated volute with dolphin head

Gable

Head-shaped keystone

Dormer window

Frieze with shell-pattern decoration

Finial

Ionic capital with head-shaped decoration

Putto holding candelabrum

Blind pediment

Grotesque figure

Medallion with bust of Robert de Montal

Lesene decorated with paterae

Frieze decorated with sculptural wreaths, tendrils, and grotesque figures

Lesene

Pedestal

Dado

Plinth | Cornice | Architrave | Portal | Pilaster

28

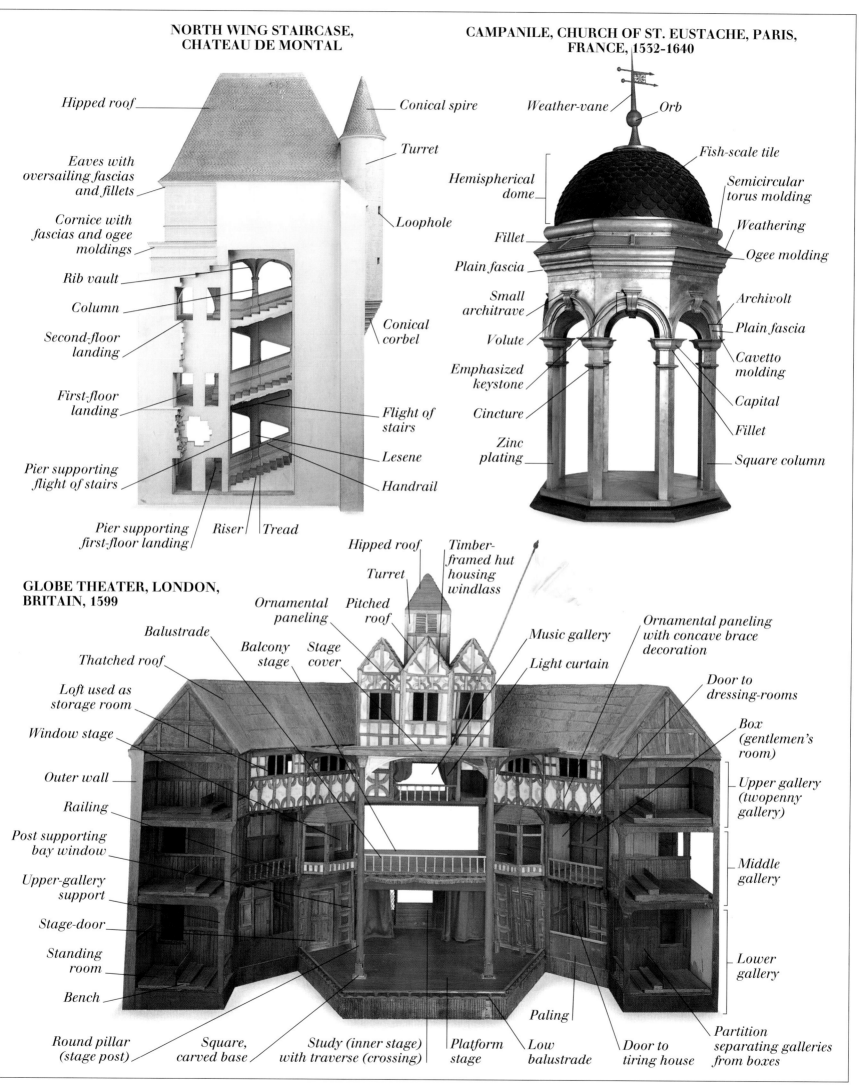

NORTH WING STAIRCASE, CHATEAU DE MONTAL

Hipped roof

Eaves with oversailing fascias and fillets

Cornice with fascias and ogee moldings

Rib vault

Column

Second-floor landing

First-floor landing

Pier supporting flight of stairs

Conical spire

Turret

Loophole

Conical corbel

Flight of stairs

Lesene

Handrail

Pier supporting first-floor landing

Riser

Tread

CAMPANILE, CHURCH OF ST. EUSTACHE, PARIS, FRANCE, 1532-1640

Weather-vane

Orb

Hemispherical dome

Fillet

Plain fascia

Small architrave

Volute

Emphasized keystone

Cincture

Zinc plating

Fish-scale tile

Semicircular torus molding

Weathering

Ogee molding

Archivolt

Plain fascia

Cavetto molding

Capital

Fillet

Square column

GLOBE THEATER, LONDON, BRITAIN, 1599

Balustrade

Thatched roof

Loft used as storage room

Window stage

Outer wall

Railing

Post supporting bay window

Upper-gallery support

Stage-door

Standing room

Bench

Round pillar (stage post)

Square, carved base

Study (inner stage) with traverse (crossing)

Hipped roof

Turret

Ornamental paneling

Balcony stage

Pitched roof

Stage cover

Timber-framed hut housing windlass

Music gallery

Light curtain

Ornamental paneling with concave brace decoration

Door to dressing-rooms

Box (gentlemen's room)

Upper gallery (twopenny gallery)

Middle gallery

Lower gallery

Partition separating galleries from boxes

Door to tiring house

Low balustrade

Platform stage

Paling

29

Baroque and neoclassical 1

THE BAROQUE STYLE EVOLVED IN THE EARLY 17TH CENTURY in Rome. It is characterized by curved outlines and ostentatious decoration, as can be seen in the Italian church details (right). The baroque style was particularly widely favored in Italy, Spain, and Germany. It was also adopted in Britain and France, but with adaptations. The British architects Christopher Wren and Nicholas Hawksmoor, for example, used baroque features—such as the concave walls of St. Paul's Cathedral and the curved buttresses of the Church of St. George in the East (see pp. 32-33)—but they did so with restraint. Similarly, the curved buttresses and volutes of the Parisian Church of St. Paul-St. Louis are relatively plain. In the second half of the 17th century, a distinct classical style (known as neoclassicism) developed in northern Europe as a reaction to the excesses of baroque. Typical of this new style were churches such as the Madeleine (a proposed facade is shown below), as well as secular buildings such as the Cirque Napoleon (opposite) and the buildings of the British architect Sir John Soane (see pp. 34-35). In early 18th century France, an extremely lavish form of baroque developed, known as rococo. The balcony from Nantes (see pp. 34-35) with its twisted ironwork and head-shaped corbels is typical of this style.

SCROLLED BUTTRESS,
CHURCH OF ST. MARIA DELLA
SALUTE, VENICE, 1631-1682

STATUE OF THE ECSTASY OF
ST. THERESA, CHURCH OF ST. MARIA
DELLA VITTORIA, ROME, 1645-1652

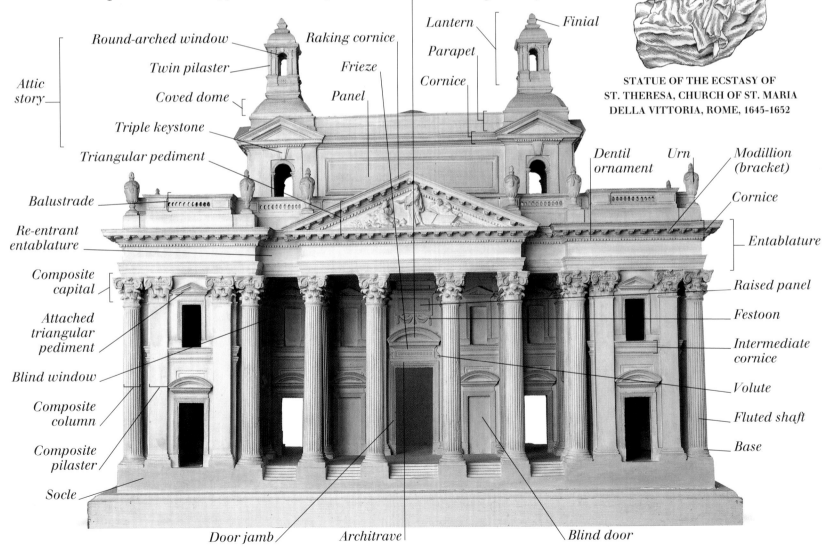

PROPOSED FACADE, THE MADELEINE (NEOCLASSICAL), PARIS, FRANCE, 1764 (BY P. CONTANT D'IVRY)

CIRQUE NAPOLEON (NEOCLASSICAL), PARIS, FRANCE, 1852 (BY J.I. HITTORFF)

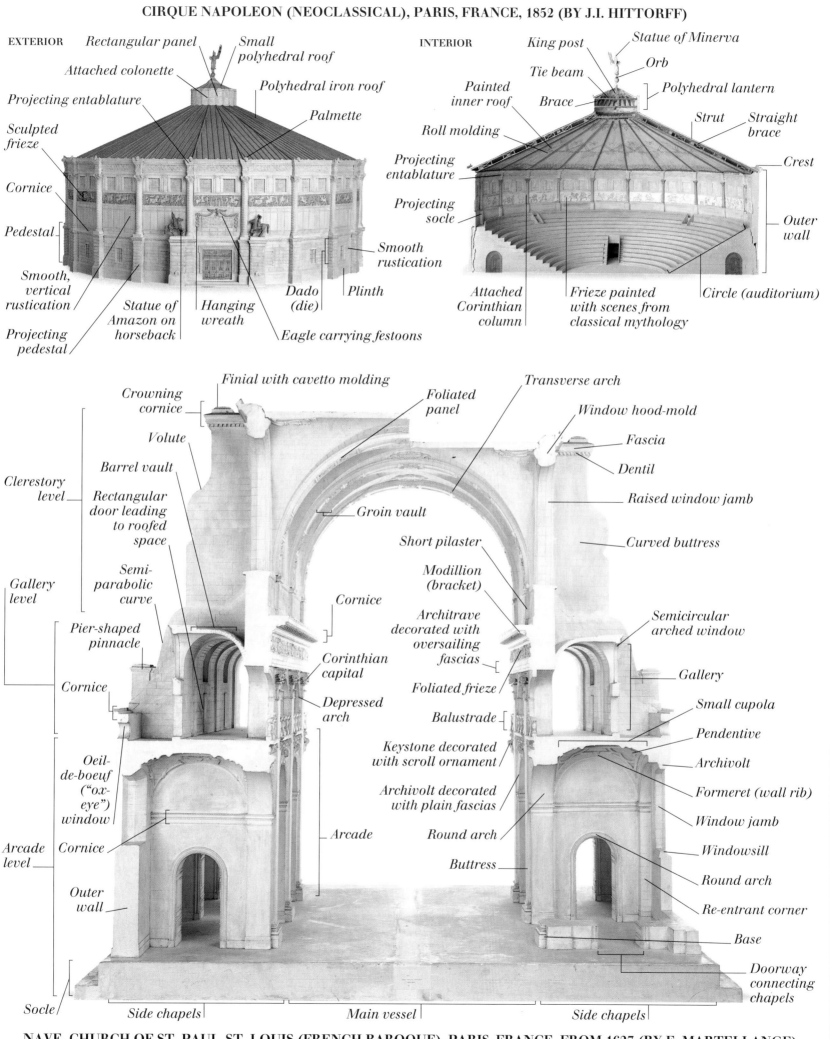

EXTERIOR

Rectangular panel

Small polyhedral roof

Attached colonette

Projecting entablature

Polyhedral iron roof

Sculpted frieze

Palmette

Cornice

Pedestal

Smooth, vertical rustication

Smooth rustication

Projecting pedestal

Statue of Amazon on horseback

Hanging wreath

Dado (die)

Plinth

Eagle carrying festoons

INTERIOR

King post

Statue of Minerva

Tie beam

Orb

Painted inner roof

Brace

Polyhedral lantern

Roll molding

Strut

Straight brace

Projecting entablature

Crest

Projecting socle

Outer wall

Attached Corinthian column

Frieze painted with scenes from classical mythology

Circle (auditorium)

Finial with cavetto molding

Transverse arch

Crowning cornice

Foliated panel

Window hood-mold

Volute

Fascia

Barrel vault

Dentil

Clerestory level

Rectangular door leading to roofed space

Groin vault

Raised window jamb

Curved buttress

Gallery level

Semi-parabolic curve

Short pilaster

Pier-shaped pinnacle

Modillion (bracket)

Semicircular arched window

Cornice

Architrave decorated with oversailing fascias

Corinthian capital

Gallery

Cornice

Depressed arch

Foliated frieze

Small cupola

Pendentive

Balustrade

Archivolt

Oeil-de-boeuf ("ox-eye") window

Keystone decorated with scroll ornament

Formeret (wall rib)

Archivolt decorated with plain fascias

Window jamb

Arcade level

Cornice

Arcade

Round arch

Windowsill

Outer wall

Buttress

Round arch

Re-entrant corner

Base

Doorway connecting chapels

Socle

Side chapels

Main vessel

Side chapels

NAVE, CHURCH OF ST. PAUL-ST. LOUIS (FRENCH BAROQUE), PARIS, FRANCE, FROM 1627 (BY E. MARTELLANGE)

Baroque and neoclassical 2

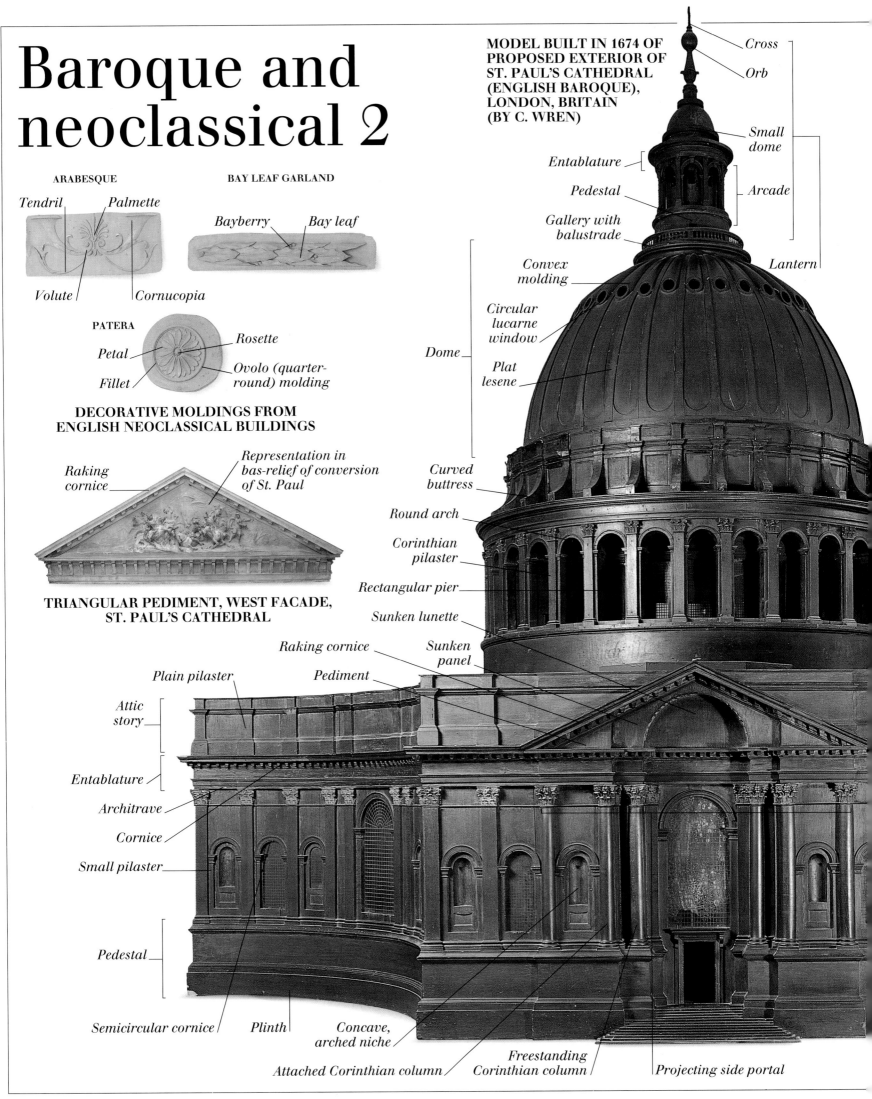

ARABESQUE

Tendril

Palmette

Volute

Cornucopia

BAY LEAF GARLAND

Bayberry

Bay leaf

PATERA

Petal

Rosette

Fillet

Ovolo (quarter-round) molding

DECORATIVE MOLDINGS FROM ENGLISH NEOCLASSICAL BUILDINGS

Raking cornice

Representation in bas-relief of conversion of St. Paul

TRIANGULAR PEDIMENT, WEST FACADE, ST. PAUL'S CATHEDRAL

MODEL BUILT IN 1674 OF PROPOSED EXTERIOR OF ST. PAUL'S CATHEDRAL (ENGLISH BAROQUE), LONDON, BRITAIN (BY C. WREN)

Cross

Orb

Small dome

Entablature

Pedestal

Arcade

Gallery with balustrade

Lantern

Convex molding

Circular lucarne window

Dome

Plat lesene

Curved buttress

Round arch

Corinthian pilaster

Rectangular pier

Sunken lunette

Raking cornice

Sunken panel

Pediment

Plain pilaster

Attic story

Entablature

Architrave

Cornice

Small pilaster

Pedestal

Semicircular cornice

Plinth

Concave, arched niche

Attached Corinthian column

Freestanding Corinthian column

Projecting side portal

CHURCH OF ST. GEORGE IN THE EAST (ENGLISH BAROQUE), LONDON, BRITAIN, 1714-1734 (BY N. HAWKSMOOR)

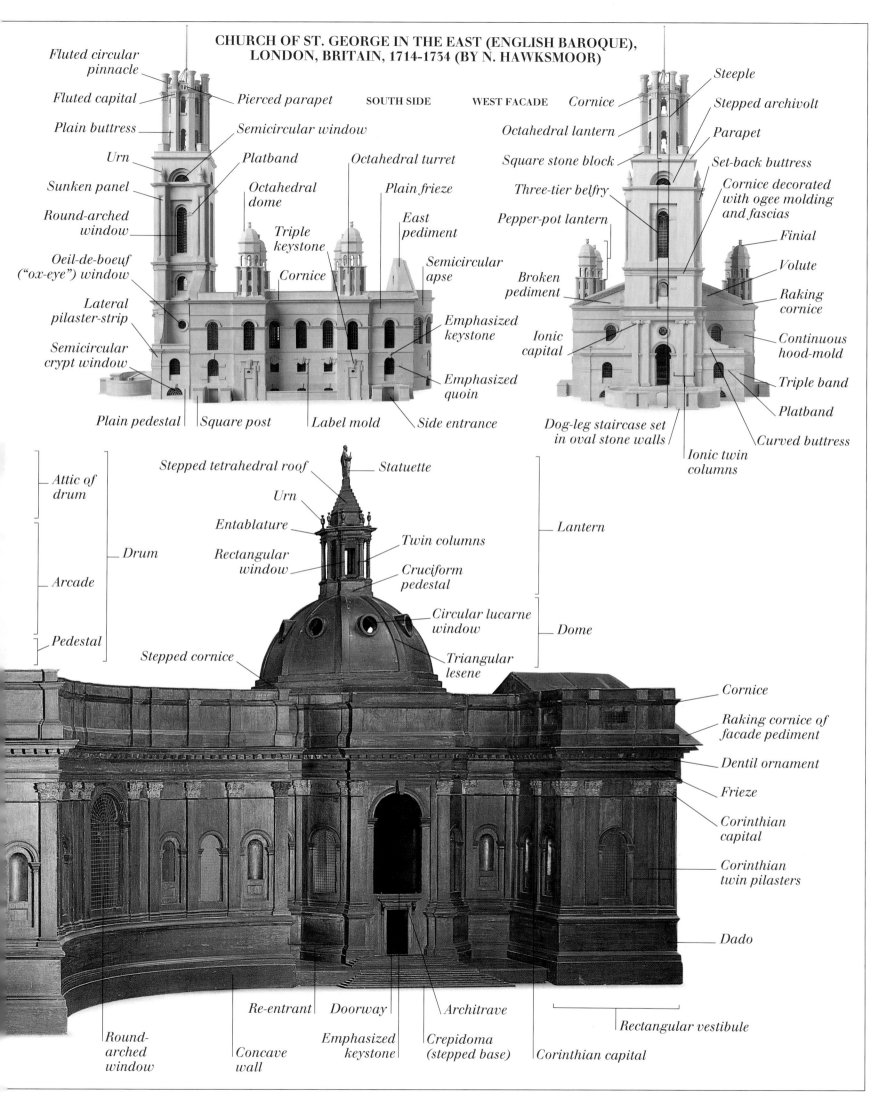

SOUTH SIDE

WEST FACADE

Fluted circular pinnacle

Fluted capital

Pierced parapet

Plain buttress

Semicircular window

Urn

Platband

Octahedral turret

Sunken panel

Octahedral dome

Plain frieze

Round-arched window

Triple keystone

East pediment

Oeil-de-boeuf ("ox-eye") window

Cornice

Semicircular apse

Lateral pilaster-strip

Emphasized keystone

Semicircular crypt window

Emphasized quoin

Plain pedestal

Square post

Label mold

Side entrance

Steeple

Cornice

Stepped archivolt

Octahedral lantern

Parapet

Square stone block

Set-back buttress

Three-tier belfry

Cornice decorated with ogee molding and fascias

Pepper-pot lantern

Finial

Broken pediment

Volute

Ionic capital

Raking cornice

Continuous hood-mold

Triple band

Dog-leg staircase set in oval stone walls

Platband

Ionic twin columns

Curved buttress

Attic of drum

Stepped tetrahedral roof

Statuette

Urn

Drum

Entablature

Twin columns

Lantern

Rectangular window

Cruciform pedestal

Arcade

Circular lucarne window

Pedestal

Dome

Stepped cornice

Triangular lesene

Cornice

Raking cornice of facade pediment

Dentil ornament

Frieze

Corinthian capital

Corinthian twin pilasters

Dado

Round-arched window

Re-entrant

Doorway

Architrave

Rectangular vestibule

Concave wall

Emphasized keystone

Crepidoma (stepped base)

Corinthian capital

Baroque and neoclassical 3

DETAILS FROM BAROQUE, NEOCLASSICAL, AND ROCOCO BUILDINGS

PORTICO, THE VYNE, HAMPSHIRE, BRITAIN, 1654 (NEOCLASSICAL)

GILT IRONWORK FROM SCREEN, PALACE OF VERSAILLES, FRANCE, 1669-1674 (FRENCH BAROQUE)

WINDOW, PALAZZO STANGA, CREMONA, ITALY, EARLY 18TH CENTURY (ROCOCO)

ATLAS (MALE CARYATID), UPPER BELVEDERE, VIENNA, AUSTRIA, 1721 (GERMAN-STYLE BAROQUE)

BALCONY, NANTES, FRANCE, 1730-1740 (ROCOCO)

MASONRY OF A NICHE IN THE ROTUNDA (NEOCLASSICAL), BANK OF ENGLAND, LONDON, BRITAIN, 1794 (BY J. SOANE)

Scoop-pattern concave molding

Keystone

Semidome

Voussoir

Rotunda wall

Frieze

Spandrel

Flat, rectangular niche

Rounded niche

Flat, square niche

CORNER OF THE NEW STATE PAPER OFFICE (NEOCLASSICAL), LONDON, BRITAIN, 1830-1831 (BY J. SOANE)

Classical-style entablature

Cornice

Frieze

Architrave

Pantile (S-shaped roofing tile)

Fascia

Eaves

Scroll-shaped corbel

Curved corbel

Second-floor window

Smooth rustication

Cornice

Drip-cap

Cornice

Frieze

Window architrave

Window jamb

First-floor window

Windowsill in the form of a frieze

Ground-floor window

Splayed windowsill

Vermiculated rustication

TYRINGHAM HOUSE (NEOCLASSICAL), BUCKINGHAMSHIRE, BRITAIN, 1793-1797 (BY J. SOANE)

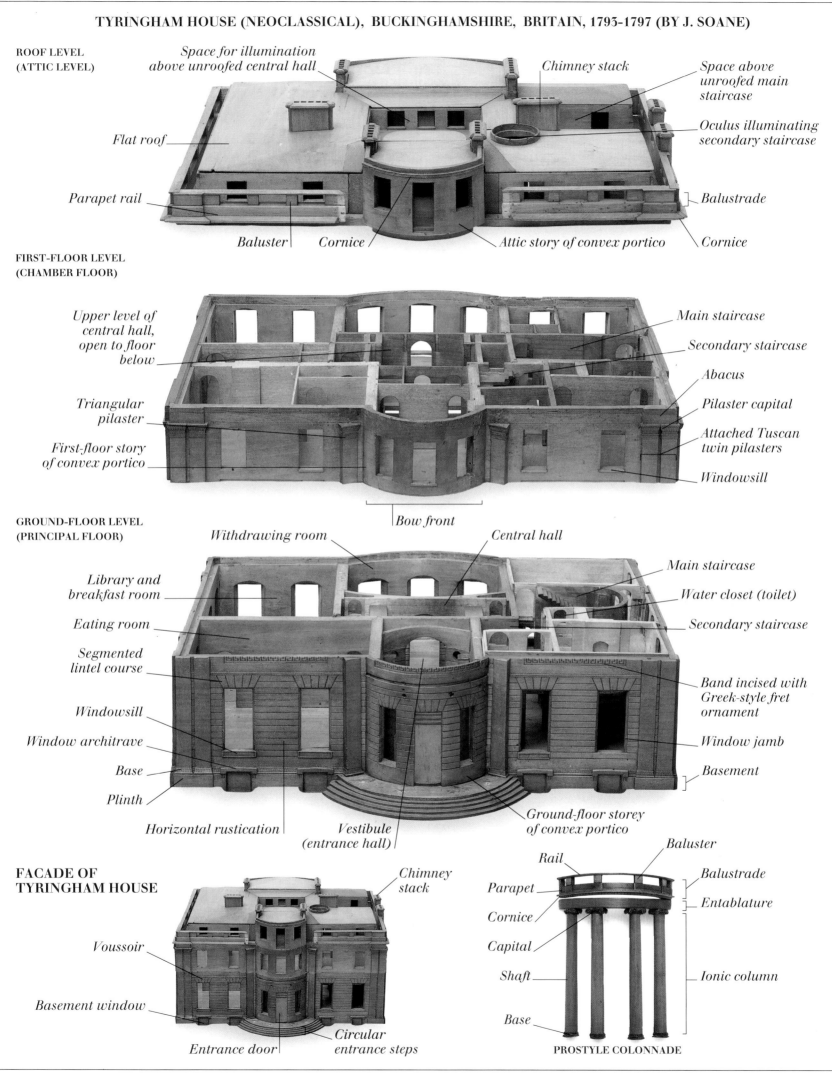

ROOF LEVEL (ATTIC LEVEL)

Space for illumination above unroofed central hall

Chimney stack

Space above unroofed main staircase

Flat roof

Oculus illuminating secondary staircase

Parapet rail

Balustrade

Baluster

Cornice

Attic story of convex portico

Cornice

FIRST-FLOOR LEVEL (CHAMBER FLOOR)

Upper level of central hall, open to floor below

Main staircase

Secondary staircase

Abacus

Pilaster capital

Triangular pilaster

First-floor story of convex portico

Attached Tuscan twin pilasters

Windowsill

Bow front

GROUND-FLOOR LEVEL (PRINCIPAL FLOOR)

Withdrawing room

Central hall

Main staircase

Library and breakfast room

Water closet (toilet)

Eating room

Secondary staircase

Segmented lintel course

Windowsill

Band incised with Greek-style fret ornament

Window architrave

Window jamb

Base

Basement

Plinth

Horizontal rustication

Vestibule (entrance hall)

Ground-floor storey of convex portico

FACADE OF TYRINGHAM HOUSE

Chimney stack

Voussoir

Basement window

Entrance door

Circular entrance steps

Rail

Baluster

Parapet

Balustrade

Cornice

Entablature

Capital

Shaft

Ionic column

Base

PROSTYLE COLONNADE

Ceilings

EARLY CEILINGS WERE SIMPLY the underside of the floor above with the timbers exposed. By the 16th century, the timbers were covered with boards and stucco (plaster). Molded stucco ceilings became popular during the 17th century. Some were elaborately ornamented, such as the one shown here. Even today, board-and-plaster ceilings are commonly used in new buildings.

Scrolled petal

Stylized stamen

PATERA (ROSETTE)

MIDDLE PANELS: TRIUMPHAL PROCESSION OF CHERUBS (TOP AND BOTTOM); GLORIFICATION OF JAMES I (CENTER)

MOLDED STUCCO CEILING, THE BANQUETING HOUSE, WHITEHALL PALACE, LONDON, BRITAIN, 1666-1693 (DESIGNED BY I. JONES, PAINTED BY P.P. RUBENS)

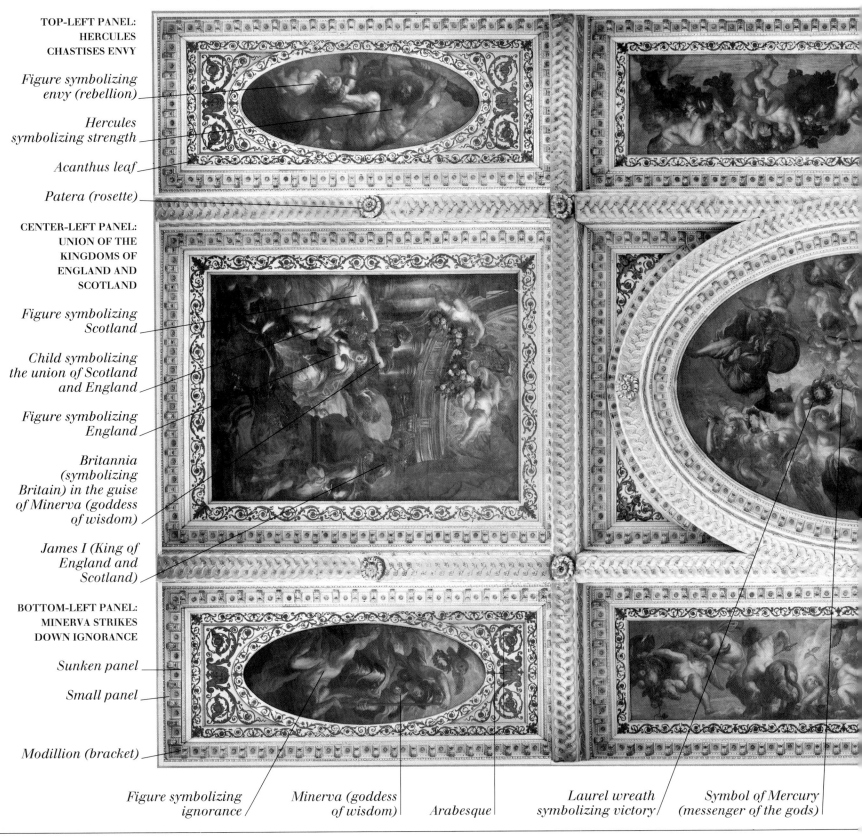

TOP-LEFT PANEL: HERCULES CHASTISES ENVY

Figure symbolizing envy (rebellion)

Hercules symbolizing strength

Acanthus leaf

Patera (rosette)

CENTER-LEFT PANEL: UNION OF THE KINGDOMS OF ENGLAND AND SCOTLAND

Figure symbolizing Scotland

Child symbolizing the union of Scotland and England

Figure symbolizing England

Britannia (symbolizing Britain) in the guise of Minerva (goddess of wisdom)

James I (King of England and Scotland)

BOTTOM-LEFT PANEL: MINERVA STRIKES DOWN IGNORANCE

Sunken panel

Small panel

Modillion (bracket)

Figure symbolizing ignorance

Minerva (goddess of wisdom)

Arabesque

Laurel wreath symbolizing victory

Symbol of Mercury (messenger of the gods)

DETAILS OF MOLDED STUCCO FROM THE BANQUETING HOUSE CEILING

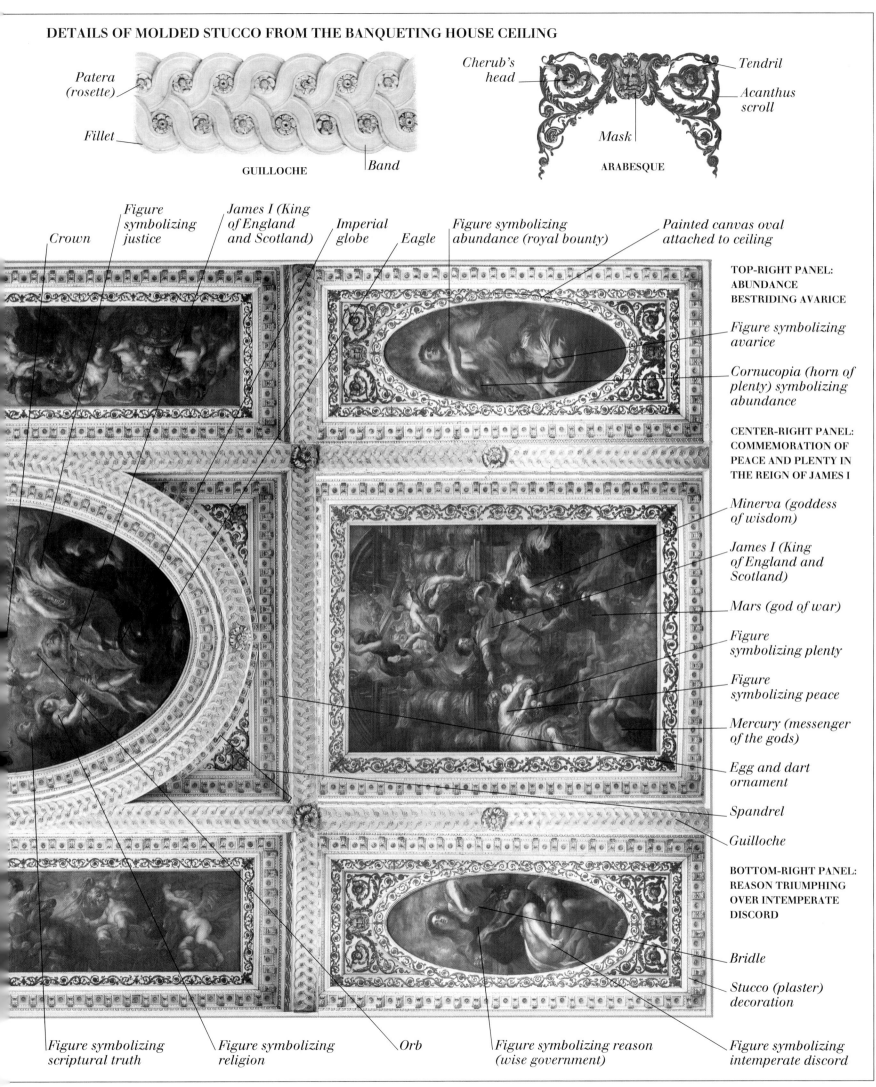

Patera (rosette)

Fillet

GUILLOCHE

Band

Cherub's head

Tendril

Acanthus scroll

Mask

ARABESQUE

Crown

Figure symbolizing justice

James I (King of England and Scotland)

Imperial globe

Eagle

Figure symbolizing abundance (royal bounty)

Painted canvas oval attached to ceiling

TOP-RIGHT PANEL: ABUNDANCE BESTRIDING AVARICE

Figure symbolizing avarice

Cornucopia (horn of plenty) symbolizing abundance

CENTER-RIGHT PANEL: COMMEMORATION OF PEACE AND PLENTY IN THE REIGN OF JAMES I

Minerva (goddess of wisdom)

James I (King of England and Scotland)

Mars (god of war)

Figure symbolizing plenty

Figure symbolizing peace

Mercury (messenger of the gods)

Egg and dart ornament

Spandrel

Guilloche

BOTTOM-RIGHT PANEL: REASON TRIUMPHING OVER INTEMPERATE DISCORD

Bridle

Stucco (plaster) decoration

Figure symbolizing scriptural truth

Figure symbolizing religion

Orb

Figure symbolizing reason (wise government)

Figure symbolizing intemperate discord

37

Arches and vaults

ARCHES ARE CURVED STRUCTURES used to bridge spans and to support the weight of upper parts of buildings, such as domes, as in St. Paul's Cathedral (below) and the historical temple (opposite). The voussoirs (wedge-shaped blocks) that form an arch (right) support each other and convert the downward force of the weight of the building into an outward force. This outward force is in turn transferred to buttresses, piers, or abutments. A vault is an arched roof or ceiling. There are four main types of vault (opposite). A barrel vault is a single vault, semicircular in cross section; a groin vault consists of two barrel vaults intersecting at right angles; a rib vault is a groin vault reinforced by ribs; and a fan vault is a rib vault in which the ribs radiate from the springing point (where the arch begins) like a fan.

PARTS OF AN ARCH

Voussoir · Keystone · Crown · Abutment

Keystone

Abutment

Extrados

Haunch

Intrados (soffit)

Impost

Intrados (soffit)

Springing point

Abutment

Abutment

Span

FRONT

SIDE

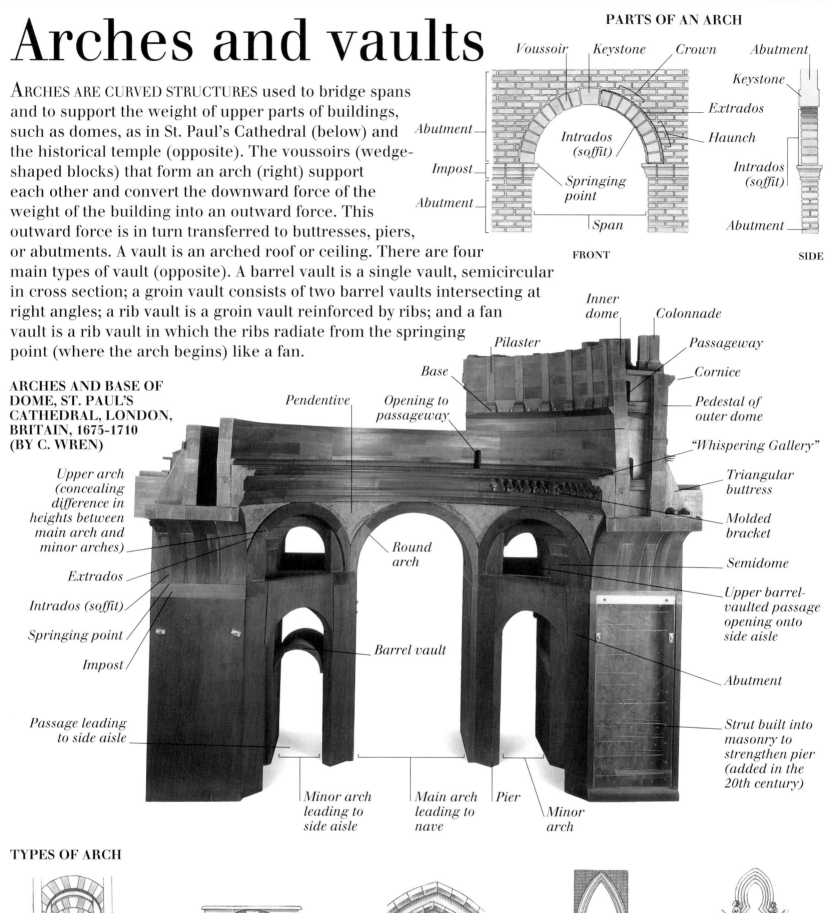

ARCHES AND BASE OF DOME, ST. PAUL'S CATHEDRAL, LONDON, BRITAIN, 1675-1710 (BY C. WREN)

Upper arch (concealing difference in heights between main arch and minor arches)

Extrados

Intrados (soffit)

Springing point

Impost

Passage leading to side aisle

Pendentive

Opening to passageway

Round arch

Barrel vault

Minor arch leading to side aisle

Main arch leading to nave

Pier

Minor arch

Inner dome

Colonnade

Pilaster

Base

Passageway

Cornice

Pedestal of outer dome

"Whispering Gallery"

Triangular buttress

Molded bracket

Semidome

Upper barrel-vaulted passage opening onto side aisle

Abutment

Strut built into masonry to strengthen pier (added in the 20th century)

TYPES OF ARCH

HORSESHOE ARCH (MOORISH ARCH), GREAT MOSQUE, CORDOBA, SPAIN, 785

BASKET ARCH (SEMI-ELLIPTICAL ARCH), PALATINE CHAPEL, AIX-LA-CHAPELLE, FRANCE, 790-798

TUDOR ARCH, TOWER OF LONDON, BRITAIN, c.1086-1097

LANCET ARCH, WESTMINSTER ABBEY, LONDON, BRITAIN, 1503-1519

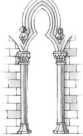

TREFOIL ARCH, BEVERLEY MINSTER, YORKSHIRE, BRITAIN, c.1300

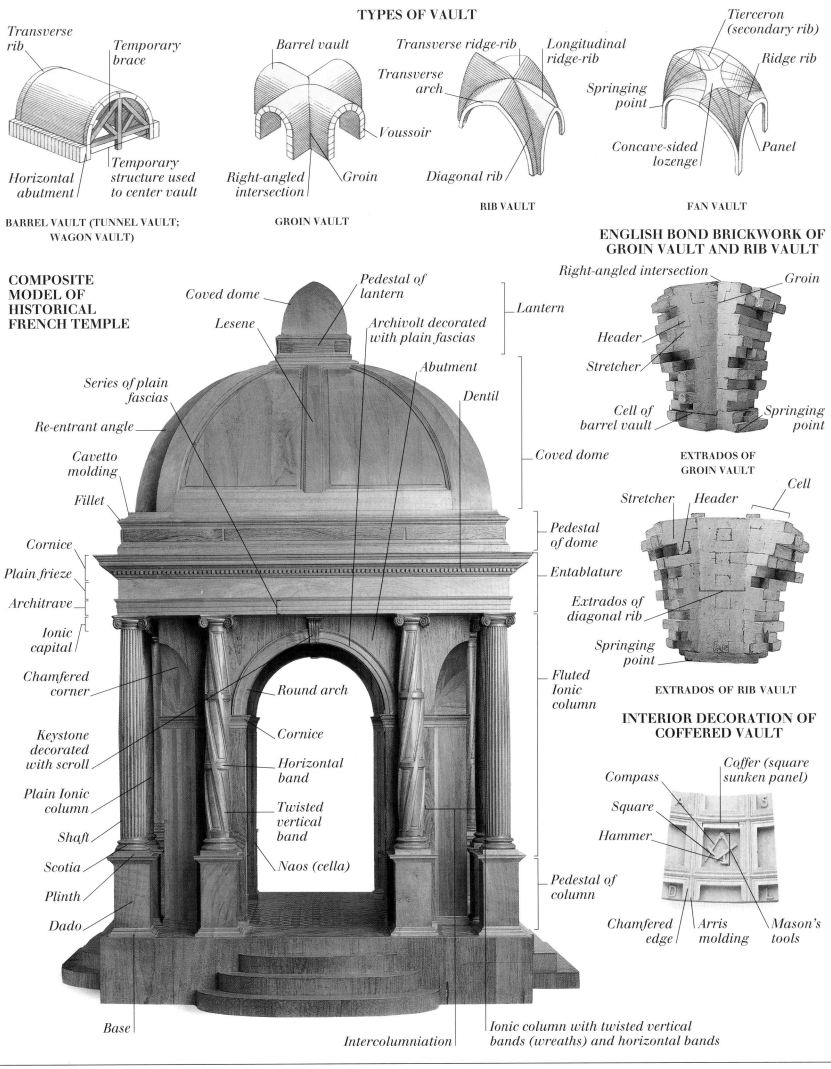

TYPES OF VAULT

Transverse rib

Temporary brace

Horizontal abutment

Temporary structure used to center vault

BARREL VAULT (TUNNEL VAULT; WAGON VAULT)

Barrel vault

Right-angled intersection

Voussoir

Groin

GROIN VAULT

Transverse ridge-rib

Longitudinal ridge-rib

Transverse arch

Diagonal rib

RIB VAULT

Tierceron (secondary rib)

Ridge rib

Springing point

Concave-sided lozenge

Panel

FAN VAULT

COMPOSITE MODEL OF HISTORICAL FRENCH TEMPLE

Coved dome

Pedestal of lantern

Lesene

Archivolt decorated with plain fascias

Lantern

Series of plain fascias

Abutment

Re-entrant angle

Dentil

Cavetto molding

Coved dome

Fillet

Cornice

Pedestal of dome

Plain frieze

Entablature

Architrave

Ionic capital

Chamfered corner

Round arch

Keystone decorated with scroll

Cornice

Plain Ionic column

Horizontal band

Shaft

Twisted vertical band

Scotia

Plinth

Naos (cella)

Dado

Fluted Ionic column

Pedestal of column

Base

Intercolumniation

Ionic column with twisted vertical bands (wreaths) and horizontal bands

ENGLISH BOND BRICKWORK OF GROIN VAULT AND RIB VAULT

Right-angled intersection

Groin

Header

Stretcher

Cell of barrel vault

Springing point

EXTRADOS OF GROIN VAULT

Stretcher

Header

Cell

Extrados of diagonal rib

Springing point

EXTRADOS OF RIB VAULT

INTERIOR DECORATION OF COFFERED VAULT

Compass

Coffer (square sunken panel)

Square

Hammer

Chamfered edge

Arris molding

Mason's tools

39

Domes

A DOME IS A CONVEX ROOF. Domes are categorized according to the shapes of both the base and the section through the center of the dome. The base may be circular, square, or polygonal (many-sided), depending on the plan of the drum (the walls on which the dome rests). The section of a dome may be the same shape as any arch (see pp. 38-39). Various types of dome are illustrated here: a hemispherical dome, which has a circular base and a semicircular section; a saucer dome, which has a circular base and a segmental (less than a semicircle) section; a polyhedral dome, which is a dome on a polygonal base whose sides meet at the top of the dome; and an onion dome, which has a circular or polygonal base and an ogee-shaped section. Many domes have a lantern (a turret with windows) to provide light inside.

LANTERN AND UPPER DOME TIMBERING, ST. PAUL'S CATHEDRAL

DOME TIMBERING, CHURCH OF THE SORBONNE, PARIS, FRANCE, 1635-1642 (BY J. LEMERCIER)

Ogee-curved dome
Straight brace
Deeply projecting pier buttress
Window zone
Cornice
Pedestal
Depressed hood mold
Circular lucarne window
Floorboard
Ashlar piece
Floor joist
Pin
Hood mold
Short strut
Waisted-oval lucarne window
Mortise and tenon joint
Principal rafter
Ogee-curved window frame
Straight brace
Vertical post
Tie beam
Circular baseplate
Common rafter
Shaft connecting lantern and church interior

ROOF WITH LANTERN AND ONION DOME

Weathercock
Ellipsoid orb
Keeled lesene
Onion dome
Fish-scale tile
Octahedral base
Oversailing fascia
Sloping roof
Round arch
Tetrahedral capital
Attached pillar
Return
Vertical band
Window
Oversailing fascia
Torus
Fillet
Octahedral base of lantern
Lantern
Tetrahedral roof

REPRESENTATION OF DOME METALING, CHURCH OF THE SORBONNE

Cross
Orb
Square rib
Inverted ovolo (quarter-round)
Astragal
Fillet
Volute
Plain fascia
Roll molding
Round-arched window
Buttress
Ovolo (quarter-round)
Volute
Lantern
Cornice
Fillet
Projecting pier buttress
Dome on a circular base
Fish-scale tile
Inverted demi-heart torus molding
Hood mold
Waisted-oval lucarne window
Small volute
Gutter
Parapet
Semicircular torus molding
Small roll
Fillet
Plain fascia
Triple lesene

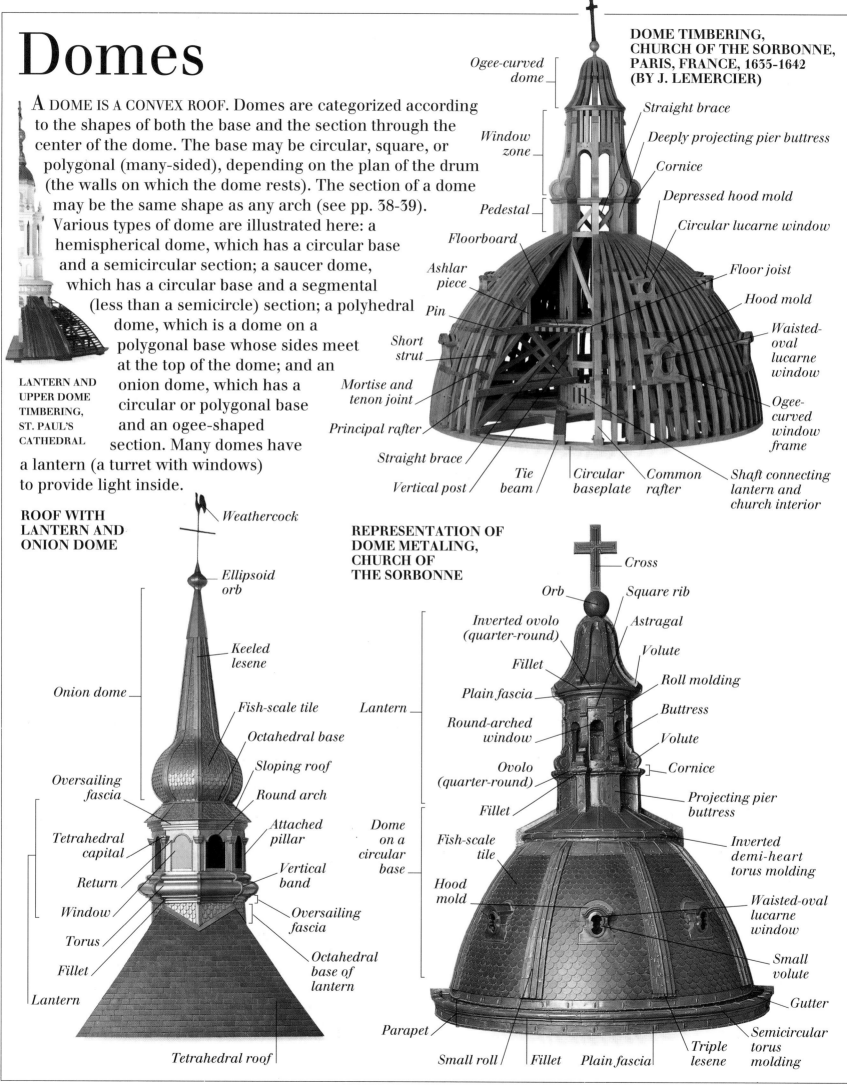

TYPES OF DOME

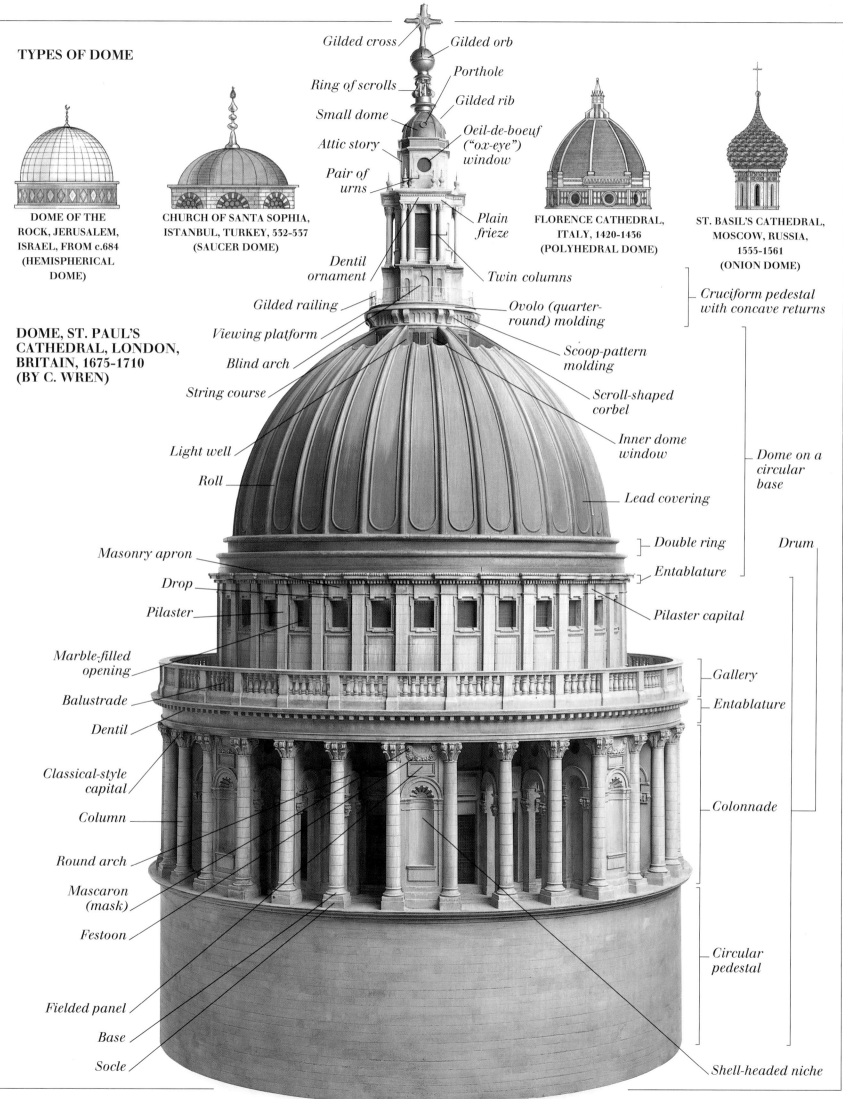

DOME OF THE ROCK, JERUSALEM, ISRAEL, FROM c.684 (HEMISPHERICAL DOME)

CHURCH OF SANTA SOPHIA, ISTANBUL, TURKEY, 532-537 (SAUCER DOME)

FLORENCE CATHEDRAL, ITALY, 1420-1436 (POLYHEDRAL DOME)

ST. BASIL'S CATHEDRAL, MOSCOW, RUSSIA, 1555-1561 (ONION DOME)

DOME, ST. PAUL'S CATHEDRAL, LONDON, BRITAIN, 1675-1710 (BY C. WREN)

Gilded cross

Gilded orb

Ring of scrolls

Porthole

Small dome

Gilded rib

Attic story

Oeil-de-boeuf ("ox-eye") window

Pair of urns

Plain frieze

Twin columns

Dentil ornament

Ovolo (quarter-round) molding

Gilded railing

Scoop-pattern molding

Viewing platform

Blind arch

Scroll-shaped corbel

String course

Inner dome window

Light well

Lead covering

Roll

Cruciform pedestal with concave returns

Dome on a circular base

Double ring

Drum

Masonry apron

Entablature

Drop

Pilaster

Pilaster capital

Marble-filled opening

Gallery

Balustrade

Entablature

Dentil

Classical-style capital

Colonnade

Column

Round arch

Mascaron (mask)

Festoon

Circular pedestal

Fielded panel

Base

Socle

Shell-headed niche

41

Islamic buildings

THE ISLAMIC RELIGION was founded by the prophet Mohammed, who was born in Mecca (in present-day Saudi Arabia) about 570 AD. During the next three centuries, Islam spread from Arabia to North Africa and Spain, as well as into India and much of the rest of Asia. The worldwide influence of Islam remains strong today. Common characteristics of Islamic buildings include ogee arches and roofs, onion domes, and walls decorated with carved stone, paintings, inlays, or mosaics. The most important type of Islamic building is the mosque—the place of worship—which generally has a minaret (tower) from which the muezzin (official crier) calls Muslims to prayer. Most mosques have a mihrab (decorative niche) that indicates the direction of Mecca. As figurative art is not allowed in Islam, buildings are ornamented with geometric and arabesque motifs and inscriptions (frequently Koranic verses).

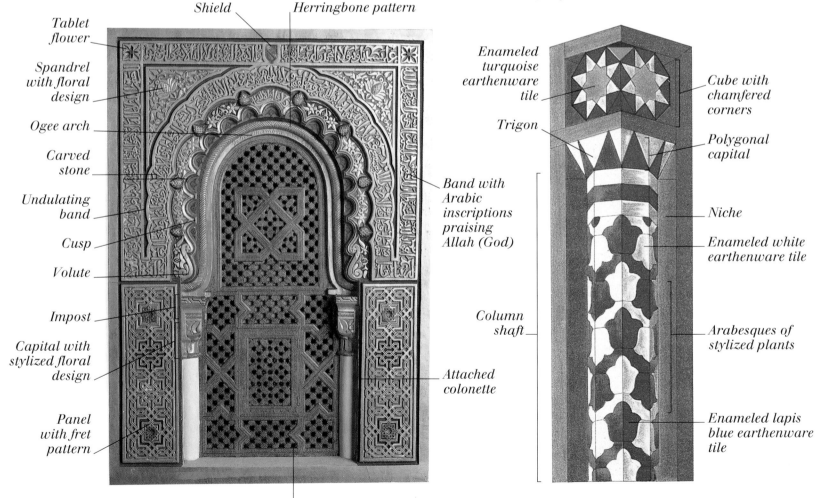

Budlike onion dome

Depressed arch surrounding mihrab

Painted roof pavilion

Turkish crescent finial

Lotus flower pendentive

Crest

Arabic inscription

Painted minaret with censer (incense burner)

Spandrel

Series of recessed arches

Semidome

Arched niche within a niche

Mural resembling tomb

Polyhedral niche

Recessed colonettes

MIHRAB, JAMI MASJID (PRINCIPAL OR CONGREGATIONAL MOSQUE), BIJAPUR, INDIA, c.1636

Tablet flower

Shield

Herringbone pattern

Spandrel with floral design

Ogee arch

Carved stone

Undulating band

Cusp

Volute

Impost

Capital with stylized floral design

Panel with fret pattern

Band with Arabic inscriptions praising Allah (God)

Attached colonette

Jali (latticed screen) with geometrical patterns

ARCH, THE ALHAMBRA, GRANADA, SPAIN, 1333-1354

Enameled turquoise earthenware tile

Trigon

Cube with chamfered corners

Polygonal capital

Column shaft

Niche

Enameled white earthenware tile

Arabesques of stylized plants

Enameled lapis blue earthenware tile

MIHRAB WITH COLUMN, EL-AINYI MOSQUE, CAIRO, EGYPT, 15TH CENTURY

EXAMPLES OF ISLAMIC MOSAICS, EGYPT AND SYRIA

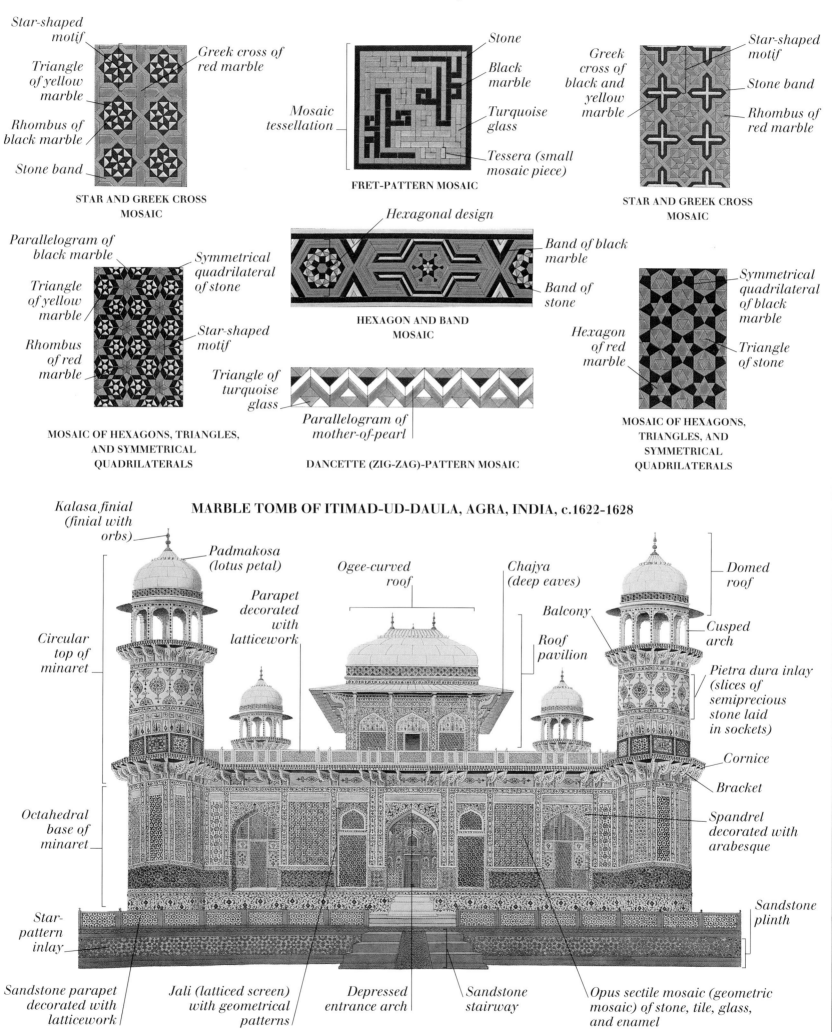

Star-shaped motif

Triangle of yellow marble

Rhombus of black marble

Stone band

Greek cross of red marble

STAR AND GREEK CROSS MOSAIC

Stone

Black marble

Turquoise glass

Mosaic tessellation

Tessera (small mosaic piece)

FRET-PATTERN MOSAIC

Greek cross of black and yellow marble

Star-shaped motif

Stone band

Rhombus of red marble

STAR AND GREEK CROSS MOSAIC

Parallelogram of black marble

Triangle of yellow marble

Rhombus of red marble

Symmetrical quadrilateral of stone

Star-shaped motif

Hexagonal design

Band of black marble

Band of stone

HEXAGON AND BAND MOSAIC

Symmetrical quadrilateral of black marble

Hexagon of red marble

Triangle of stone

MOSAIC OF HEXAGONS, TRIANGLES, AND SYMMETRICAL QUADRILATERALS

Triangle of turquoise glass

Parallelogram of mother-of-pearl

DANCETTE (ZIG-ZAG)-PATTERN MOSAIC

MOSAIC OF HEXAGONS, TRIANGLES, AND SYMMETRICAL QUADRILATERALS

MARBLE TOMB OF ITIMAD-UD-DAULA, AGRA, INDIA, c.1622–1628

Kalasa finial (finial with orbs)

Padmakosa (lotus petal)

Ogee-curved roof

Parapet decorated with latticework

Chajya (deep eaves)

Balcony

Roof pavilion

Domed roof

Circular top of minaret

Cusped arch

Pietra dura inlay (slices of semiprecious stone laid in sockets)

Octahedral base of minaret

Cornice

Bracket

Spandrel decorated with arabesque

Star-pattern inlay

Sandstone plinth

Sandstone parapet decorated with latticework

Jali (latticed screen) with geometrical patterns

Depressed entrance arch

Sandstone stairway

Opus sectile mosaic (geometric mosaic) of stone, tile, glass, and enamel

South and east Asia

THE TRADITIONAL ARCHITECTURE of south and east Asia has been profoundly influenced by the spread from India of Buddhism and Hinduism. This influence is shown by both the abundance and by the architectural styles of temples and shrines in the region. Many early Hindu temples consist of rooms carved from solid rock faces. However, freestanding structures began to be built in southern India from about the eighth century AD. Many were built in the Dravidian style, like the Temple of Virupaksha (opposite), with its characteristic antarala (terraced tower), perforated windows, and numerous arches, pilasters, and carvings. The earliest Buddhist religious monuments were Indian stupas (see pp. 58-59), which consisted of a single hemispherical dome surmounted by a chattravali (shaft) and surrounded by railings with ornate gates. Later Indian stupas and those built elsewhere were sometimes modified. For example, in Sri Lanka, the dome became bell-shaped, and was called a dagoba. Buddhist pagodas, such as the Burmese example (right), are multistoried temples, each story having a projecting roof. The form of these buildings probably derived from the yasti (pointed spire) of the stupa. Another feature of many traditional Asian buildings is their imaginative roof forms, such as gambrel (mansard) roofs, and roofs with angle rafters (below).

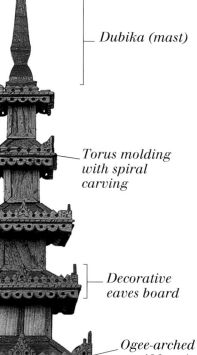

Gilded band

Gilded iron hti (crown)

Dubika (mast)

Arrow motif

Torus molding with spiral carving

Decorative eaves board

Ogee-arched motif forming horn

Ogee-arched motif with decorative carvings

Hip rafter

Pentroof

Undulating molding

Engaged pillar

Baluster finial

Arched entrance

Balustrade

Rectangular window

Pillar

Baluster

Straight brace

DETAILS FROM EAST ASIAN BUILDINGS

KASUGA-STYLE ROOF WITH SUMIGI (ANGLE RAFTERS), KASUGADO SHRINE OF ENJOJI, NARA, JAPAN, 12TH-14TH CENTURY

TERRACES, TEMPLE OF HEAVEN, BEIJING, CHINA, 15TH CENTURY

GAMBREL (MANSARD) ROOF WITH UPSWEPT EAVES AND UNDULATING GABLES, HIMEJI CASTLE, HIMEJI, JAPAN, 1608-1609

CORNER CAPITAL WITH ROOF BEAMS, POPCHU-SA TEMPLE, POPCHU-SA, SOUTH KOREA, 17TH CENTURY

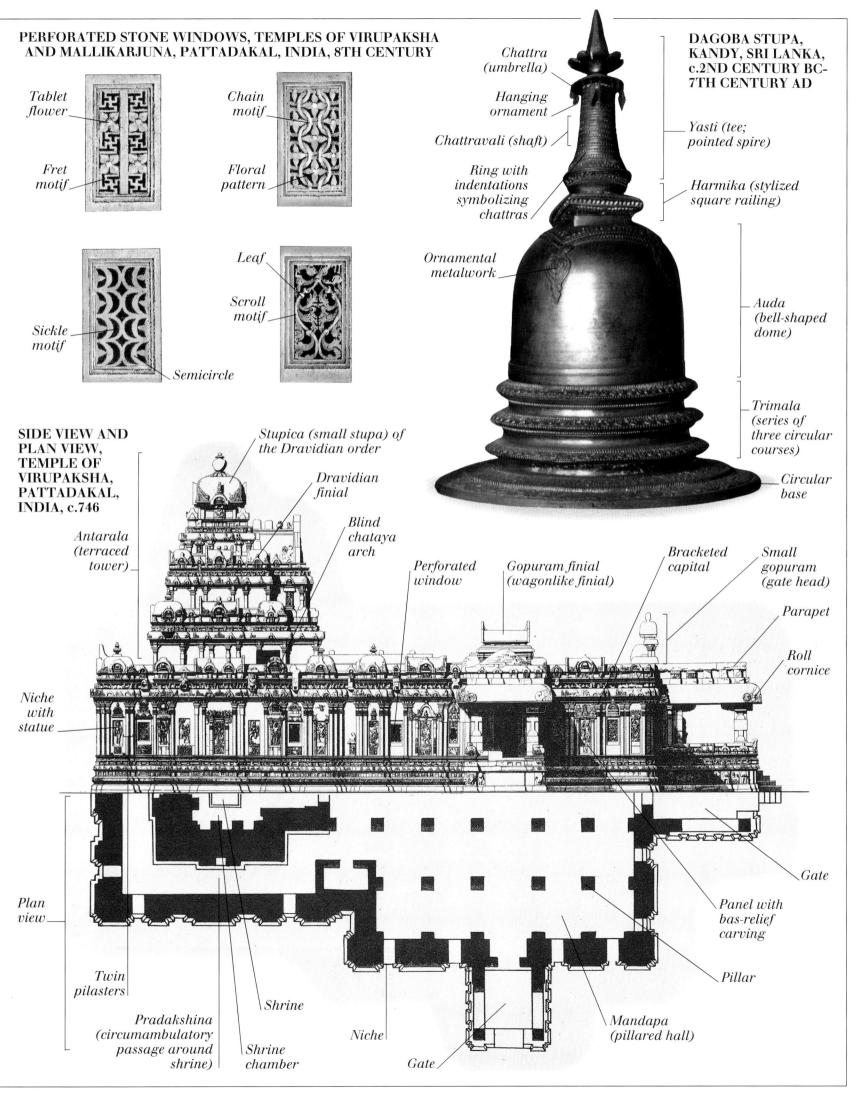

PERFORATED STONE WINDOWS, TEMPLES OF VIRUPAKSHA AND MALLIKARJUNA, PATTADAKAL, INDIA, 8TH CENTURY

Tablet flower

Fret motif

Chain motif

Floral pattern

Leaf

Scroll motif

Sickle motif

Semicircle

DAGOBA STUPA, KANDY, SRI LANKA, c.2ND CENTURY BC–7TH CENTURY AD

Chattra (umbrella)

Hanging ornament

Chattravali (shaft)

Ring with indentations symbolizing chattras

Ornamental metalwork

Yasti (tee; pointed spire)

Harmika (stylized square railing)

Auda (bell-shaped dome)

Trimala (series of three circular courses)

Circular base

SIDE VIEW AND PLAN VIEW, TEMPLE OF VIRUPAKSHA, PATTADAKAL, INDIA, c.746

Stupica (small stupa) of the Dravidian order

Dravidian finial

Blind chataya arch

Antarala (terraced tower)

Niche with statue

Perforated window

Gopuram finial (wagonlike finial)

Bracketed capital

Small gopuram (gate head)

Parapet

Roll cornice

Gate

Panel with bas-relief carving

Pillar

Plan view

Twin pilasters

Pradakshina (circumambulatory passage around shrine)

Shrine

Shrine chamber

Niche

Mandapa (pillared hall)

Gate

Doors

A DOOR AND ITS SURROUNDING FRAME make up a doorway. Doorways that are particularly grand or imposing are known as portals, examples of which include the portals of Lund and Cologne cathedrals (opposite). There are two main types of door, paneled and matchboarded, both of which were used as long ago as ancient Egyptian times. Paneled doors consist of a frame of horizontal rails and vertical muntins, with infilled panels of wood or glass. Matchboarded doors consist of long vertical boards held in position by horizontal rails and diagonal braces.

PARTS OF A PANELED DOOR

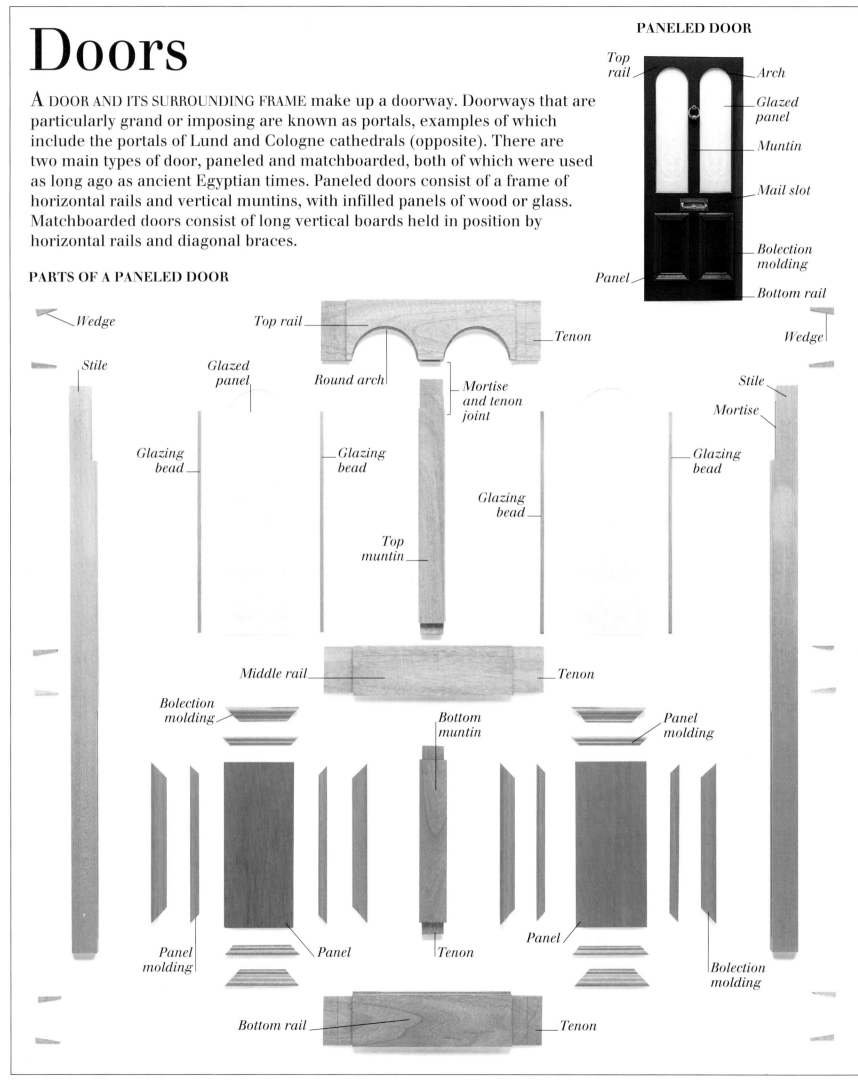

Top rail · *Arch* · *Glazed panel* · *Muntin* · *Mail slot* · *Bolection molding* · *Panel* · *Bottom rail*

Wedge · *Top rail* · *Tenon* · *Wedge*

Stile · *Glazed panel* · *Round arch* · *Mortise and tenon joint* · *Stile* · *Mortise*

Glazing bead · *Glazing bead* · *Glazing bead* · *Glazing bead*

Top muntin

Middle rail · *Tenon*

Bolection molding · *Bottom muntin* · *Panel molding*

Panel molding · *Panel* · *Tenon* · *Panel* · *Bolection molding*

Bottom rail · *Tenon*

TYPES OF DOOR

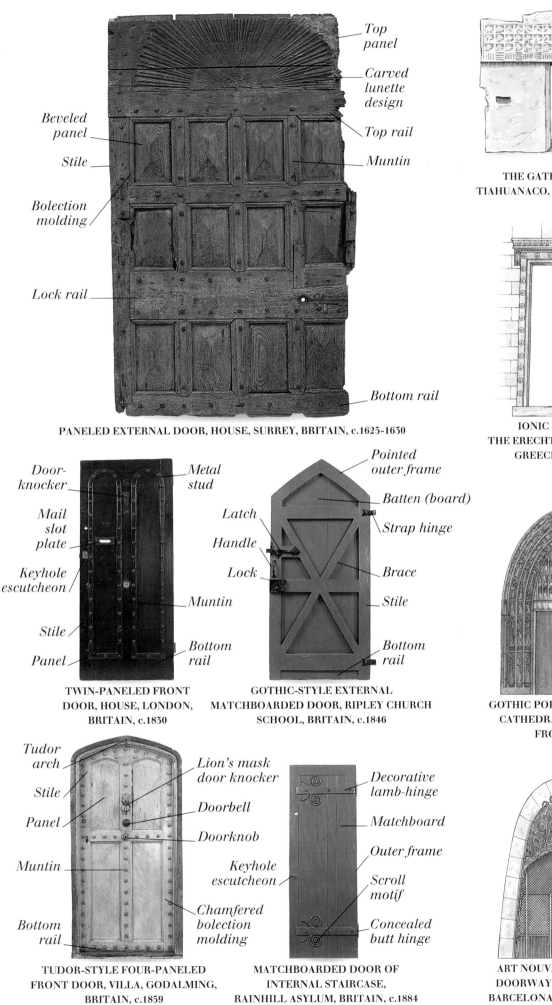

PANELED EXTERNAL DOOR, HOUSE, SURREY, BRITAIN, c.1625-1630

Top panel

Carved lunette design

Beveled panel

Top rail

Stile

Muntin

Bolection molding

Lock rail

Bottom rail

Door-knocker

Metal stud

Mail slot plate

Keyhole escutcheon

Muntin

Stile

Panel

Bottom rail

TWIN-PANELED FRONT DOOR, HOUSE, LONDON, BRITAIN, c.1830

Pointed outer frame

Batten (board)

Latch

Strap hinge

Handle

Lock

Brace

Stile

Bottom rail

GOTHIC-STYLE EXTERNAL MATCHBOARDED DOOR, RIPLEY CHURCH SCHOOL, BRITAIN, c.1846

Tudor arch

Lion's mask door knocker

Stile

Doorbell

Panel

Doorknob

Muntin

Keyhole escutcheon

Bottom rail

Chamfered bolection molding

TUDOR-STYLE FOUR-PANELED FRONT DOOR, VILLA, GODALMING, BRITAIN, c.1859

Decorative lamb-hinge

Matchboard

Outer frame

Scroll motif

Concealed butt hinge

MATCHBOARDED DOOR OF INTERNAL STAIRCASE, RAINHILL ASYLUM, BRITAIN, c.1884

TYPES OF DOORWAY AND PORTAL

THE GATE OF THE SUN, TIAHUANACO, BOLIVIA, c.600-1000

ANGLO-SAXON TRIANGULAR-ARCHED DOORWAY, BRITAIN, c.900

IONIC DOORWAY, THE ERECHTHEION, ATHENS, GREECE, 421-405 BC

ROMANESQUE PORTAL, LUND CATHEDRAL, SWEDEN, FROM c.1103

GOTHIC PORTAL, COLOGNE CATHEDRAL, GERMANY, FROM 1248

RENAISSANCE DOORWAY, CHURCH OF ST. ZACCARIA, VENICE, ITALY, FROM 1485

ART NOUVEAU ELLIPSOID DOORWAY, PALAU GÜELL, BARCELONA, SPAIN, 1885-1889

ART DECO ELEVATOR DOORS, CHRYSLER BUILDING, NEW YORK, USA, 1928-1930

Windows

THE EARLIEST windows were simply openings for light and ventilation. Glazed windows were first used by the ancient Romans, but they did not appear often in domestic houses until the 16th century. Early glazing consisted of quarrels (small panes of glass) held together by cames (lead strips) to form a light. As windows became larger, the individual lights were joined together by horizontal transoms and vertical mullions. Casement windows and sash windows originated in the 16th and 17th centuries. A casement window can be swung open on a hinge attached to the side of the window frame, whereas a sash window slides up and down on a sash cord attached, by a pulley, to a weight. The development of metal frames—as in the Bauhaus windows at Dessau, Germany—and the availability of large panes of glass eventually made it possible to cover buildings almost entirely with glass.

OEIL-DE-BOEUF ("OX-EYE") WINDOW

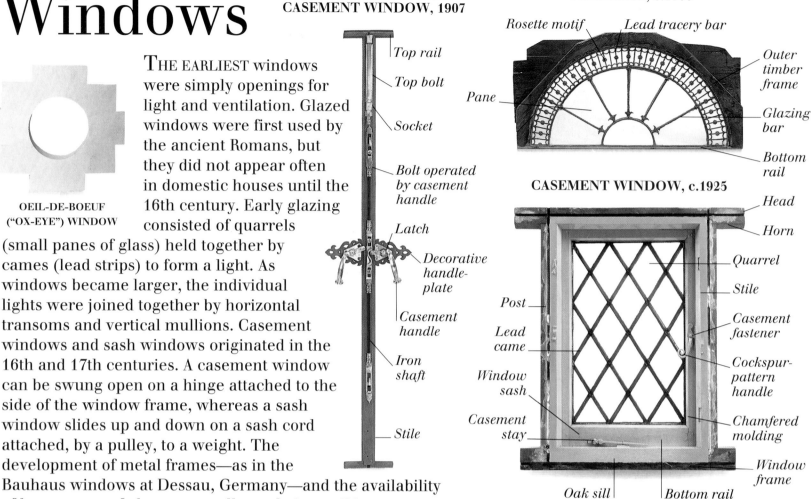

SECTION FROM STEEL CASEMENT WINDOW, 1907

Top rail
Top bolt
Socket
Bolt operated by casement handle
Latch
Decorative handle-plate
Casement handle
Iron shaft
Stile

FANLIGHT, c.1700

Rosette motif
Lead tracery bar
Outer timber frame
Pane
Glazing bar
Bottom rail

CASEMENT WINDOW, c.1925

Head
Horn
Quarrel
Stile
Casement fastener
Cockspur-pattern handle
Chamfered molding
Window frame
Post
Lead came
Window sash
Casement stay
Oak sill
Bottom rail

STAINED GLASS (DETAILS) FROM THE ROYAL COURTS OF JUSTICE, LONDON, BRITAIN, 1866

Coat of arms
Lead came
Quarrel
Circular quarrel
Diaper work (background design)
Rectangular quarrel

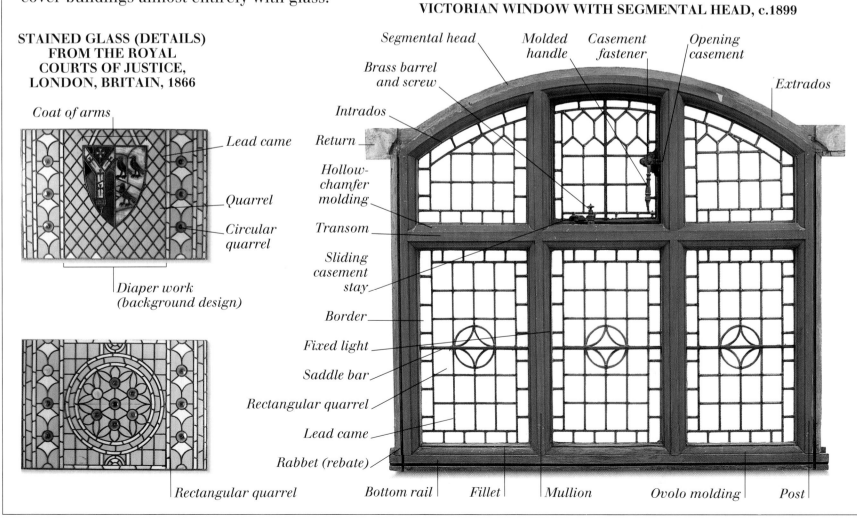

VICTORIAN WINDOW WITH SEGMENTAL HEAD, c.1899

Segmental head
Molded handle
Casement fastener
Opening casement
Brass barrel and screw
Extrados
Intrados
Return
Hollow-chamfer molding
Transom
Sliding casement stay
Border
Fixed light
Saddle bar
Rectangular quarrel
Lead came
Rabbet (rebate)
Bottom rail
Fillet
Mullion
Ovolo molding
Post

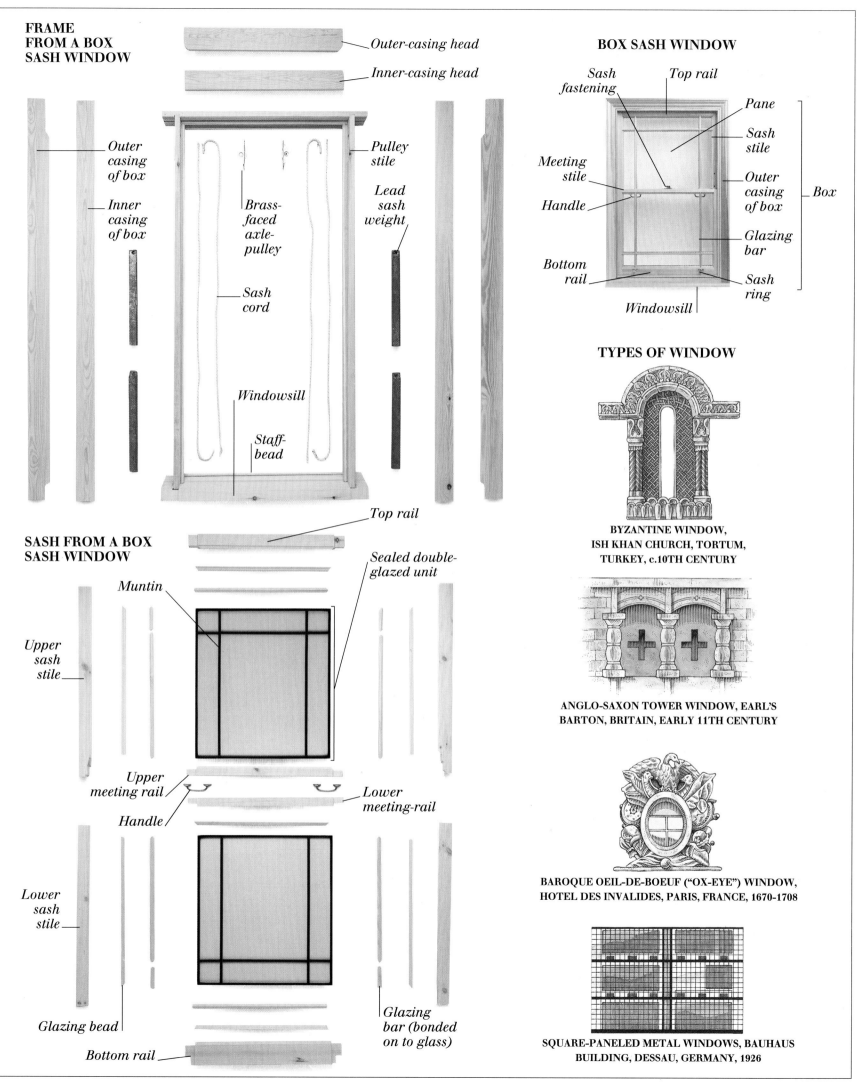

FRAME FROM A BOX SASH WINDOW

Outer-casing head

Inner-casing head

Outer casing of box

Inner casing of box

Brass-faced axle-pulley

Sash cord

Windowsill

Staff-bead

Pulley stile

Lead sash weight

BOX SASH WINDOW

Sash fastening

Top rail

Pane

Sash stile

Meeting stile

Handle

Outer casing of box

Glazing bar

Bottom rail

Sash ring

Box

Windowsill

TYPES OF WINDOW

BYZANTINE WINDOW, ISH KHAN CHURCH, TORTUM, TURKEY, c.10TH CENTURY

ANGLO-SAXON TOWER WINDOW, EARL'S BARTON, BRITAIN, EARLY 11TH CENTURY

BAROQUE OEIL-DE-BOEUF ("OX-EYE") WINDOW, HOTEL DES INVALIDES, PARIS, FRANCE, 1670-1708

SQUARE-PANELED METAL WINDOWS, BAUHAUS BUILDING, DESSAU, GERMANY, 1926

SASH FROM A BOX SASH WINDOW

Top rail

Sealed double-glazed unit

Muntin

Upper sash stile

Upper meeting rail

Handle

Lower meeting-rail

Lower sash stile

Glazing bar (bonded on to glass)

Glazing bead

Bottom rail

The 19th century

BUILDINGS OF THE 19TH CENTURY are characterized by the use of new materials and by a great diversity of architectural styles. From the end of the 18th century, iron and steel became widely used as an alternative to wood for the framework of buildings, as in the flax-spinning mill shown here. Built in Britain in 1796, this mill exemplifies an architectural style that became common throughout the industrialized world for more than a century. The Industrial Revolution also brought mass production of building parts—a development that enabled the British architect Sir Joseph Paxton to erect London's Crystal Palace (a building made entirely of iron and glass) in only nine months, ready for the Great Exhibition of 1851. The 19th century saw a widespread revival of older architectural styles. For example, in the United States and Germany, Neo-Greek architecture was fashionable; in Britain and France, Neo-Baroque, Neo-Byzantine, and Neo-Gothic styles (as seen in the Palace of Westminster and Tower Bridge, London) were dominant.

FLAX-SPINNING MILL, SHREWSBURY, BRITAIN, 1796 (BY C. BAGE)

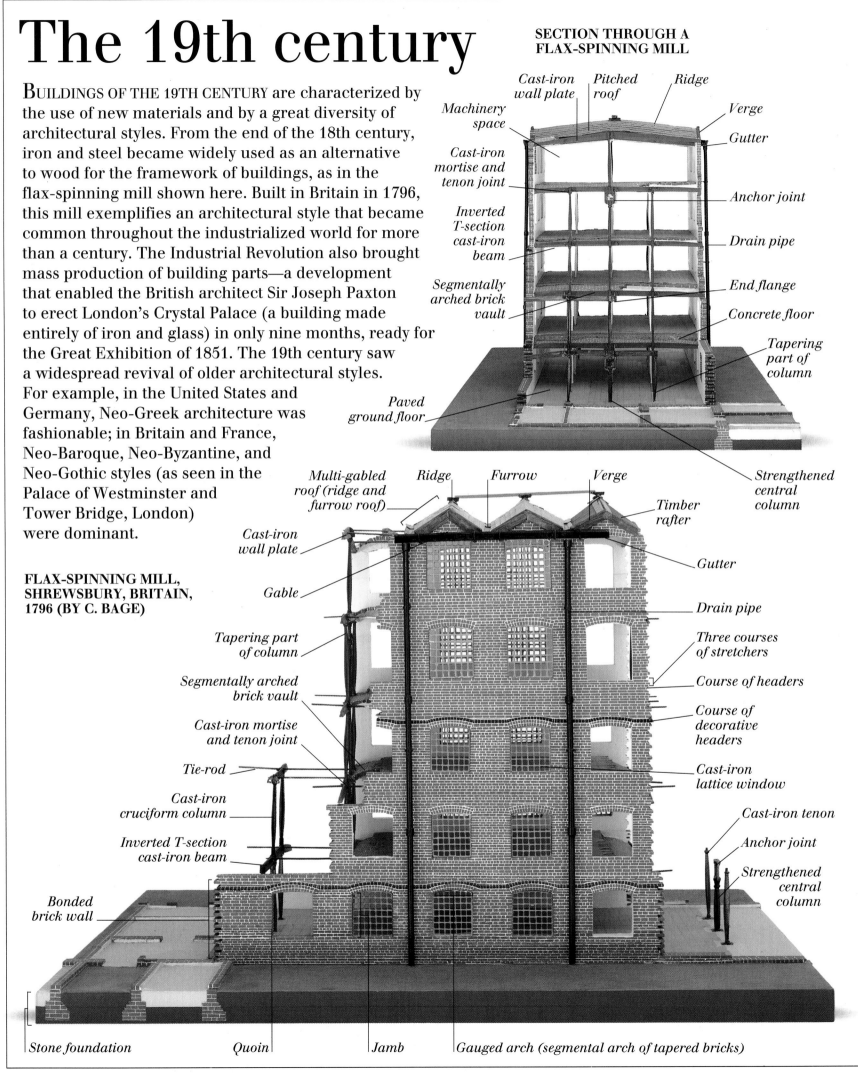

Cast-iron wall plate
Pitched roof
Ridge
Verge
Machinery space
Gutter
Cast-iron mortise and tenon joint
Anchor joint
Inverted T-section cast-iron beam
Drain pipe
Segmentally arched brick vault
End flange
Concrete floor
Tapering part of column
Paved ground floor
Strengthened central column

Multi-gabled roof (ridge and furrow roof)
Ridge
Furrow
Verge
Cast-iron wall plate
Timber rafter
Gable
Gutter
Tapering part of column
Drain pipe
Segmentally arched brick vault
Three courses of stretchers
Cast-iron mortise and tenon joint
Course of headers
Tie-rod
Course of decorative headers
Cast-iron cruciform column
Cast-iron lattice window
Inverted T-section cast-iron beam
Cast-iron tenon
Anchor joint
Strengthened central column
Bonded brick wall

Stone foundation
Quoin
Jamb
Gauged arch (segmental arch of tapered bricks)

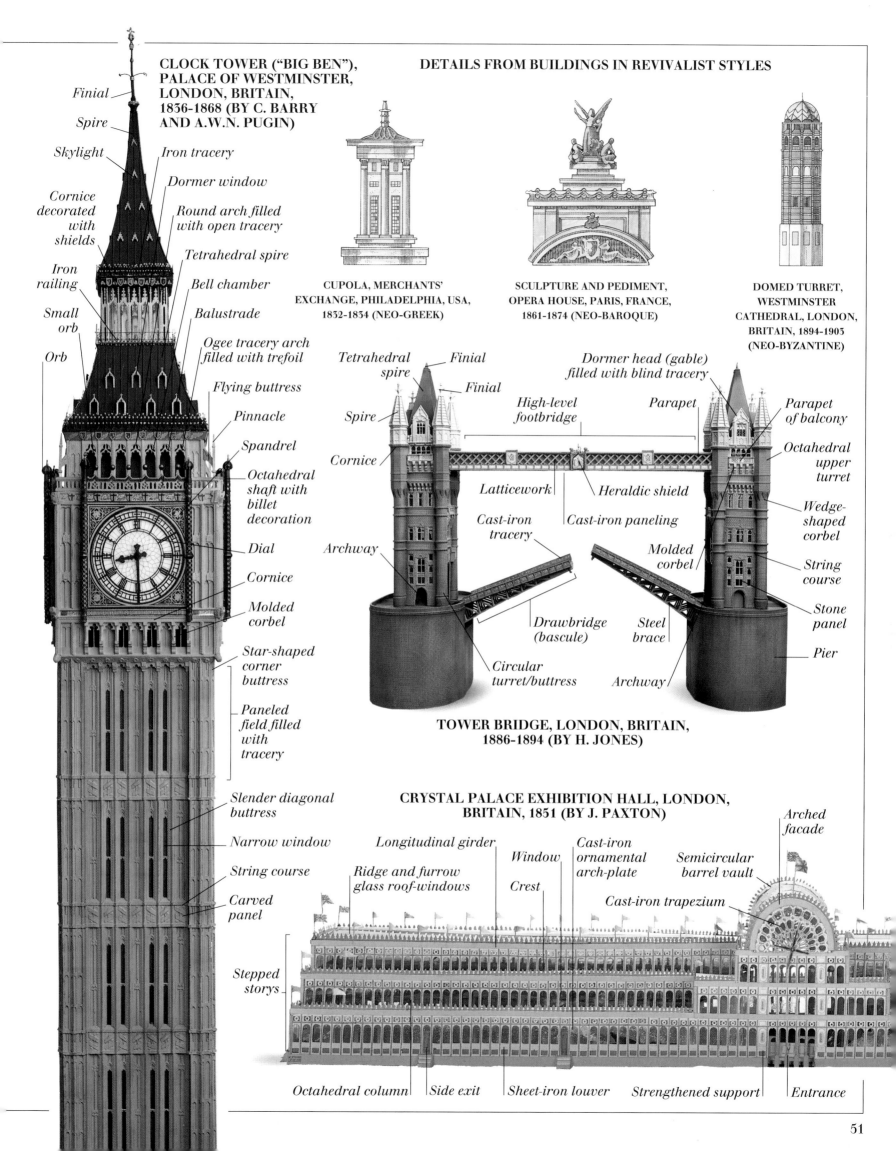

CLOCK TOWER ("BIG BEN"), PALACE OF WESTMINSTER, LONDON, BRITAIN, 1836-1868 (BY C. BARRY AND A.W.N. PUGIN)

Finial
Spire
Skylight
Cornice decorated with shields
Iron railing
Small orb
Orb
Iron tracery
Dormer window
Round arch filled with open tracery
Tetrahedral spire
Bell chamber
Balustrade
Ogee tracery arch filled with trefoil
Flying buttress
Pinnacle
Spandrel
Octahedral shaft with billet decoration
Dial
Cornice
Molded corbel
Star-shaped corner buttress
Paneled field filled with tracery
Slender diagonal buttress
Narrow window
String course
Carved panel

DETAILS FROM BUILDINGS IN REVIVALIST STYLES

CUPOLA, MERCHANTS' EXCHANGE, PHILADELPHIA, USA, 1832-1834 (NEO-GREEK)

SCULPTURE AND PEDIMENT, OPERA HOUSE, PARIS, FRANCE, 1861-1874 (NEO-BAROQUE)

DOMED TURRET, WESTMINSTER CATHEDRAL, LONDON, BRITAIN, 1894-1903 (NEO-BYZANTINE)

TOWER BRIDGE, LONDON, BRITAIN, 1886-1894 (BY H. JONES)

Tetrahedral spire
Finial
Finial
Spire
Cornice
Archway
High-level footbridge
Latticework
Cast-iron tracery
Dormer head (gable) filled with blind tracery
Parapet
Heraldic shield
Cast-iron paneling
Molded corbel
Drawbridge (bascule)
Steel brace
Circular turret/buttress
Archway
Parapet of balcony
Octahedral upper turret
Wedge-shaped corbel
String course
Stone panel
Pier

CRYSTAL PALACE EXHIBITION HALL, LONDON, BRITAIN, 1851 (BY J. PAXTON)

Longitudinal girder
Ridge and furrow glass roof-windows
Window
Crest
Cast-iron ornamental arch-plate
Semicircular barrel vault
Cast-iron trapezium
Arched facade
Stepped storys
Octahedral column
Side exit
Sheet-iron louver
Strengthened support
Entrance

The early 20th century

ARCHITECTURE OF THE EARLY 20TH CENTURY is notable for radical new types of steel and glass buildings—particularly skyscrapers—and the widespread use of steel-reinforced concrete. The steel-framed skyscraper was pioneered in Chicago in the 1880s but did not become widespread until the first decades of the 20th century. As construction techniques were refined, skyscrapers became higher and higher. For example, the Empire State Building (right) of 1929-1931 has 102 storys. Many buildings of this period were constructed from lightweight concrete slabs that could be supported by cantilever beams or by pilotis (stilts), as in the Villa Savoye (below). The early 20th century also produced a great variety of architectural styles, some of which are illustrated opposite. Despite their diversity, the styles of this period generally had one thing in common: they were completely new, with few links to past architectural styles. This originality is in marked contrast to 19th-century architecture (see pp. 50-51), much of which was revivalist.

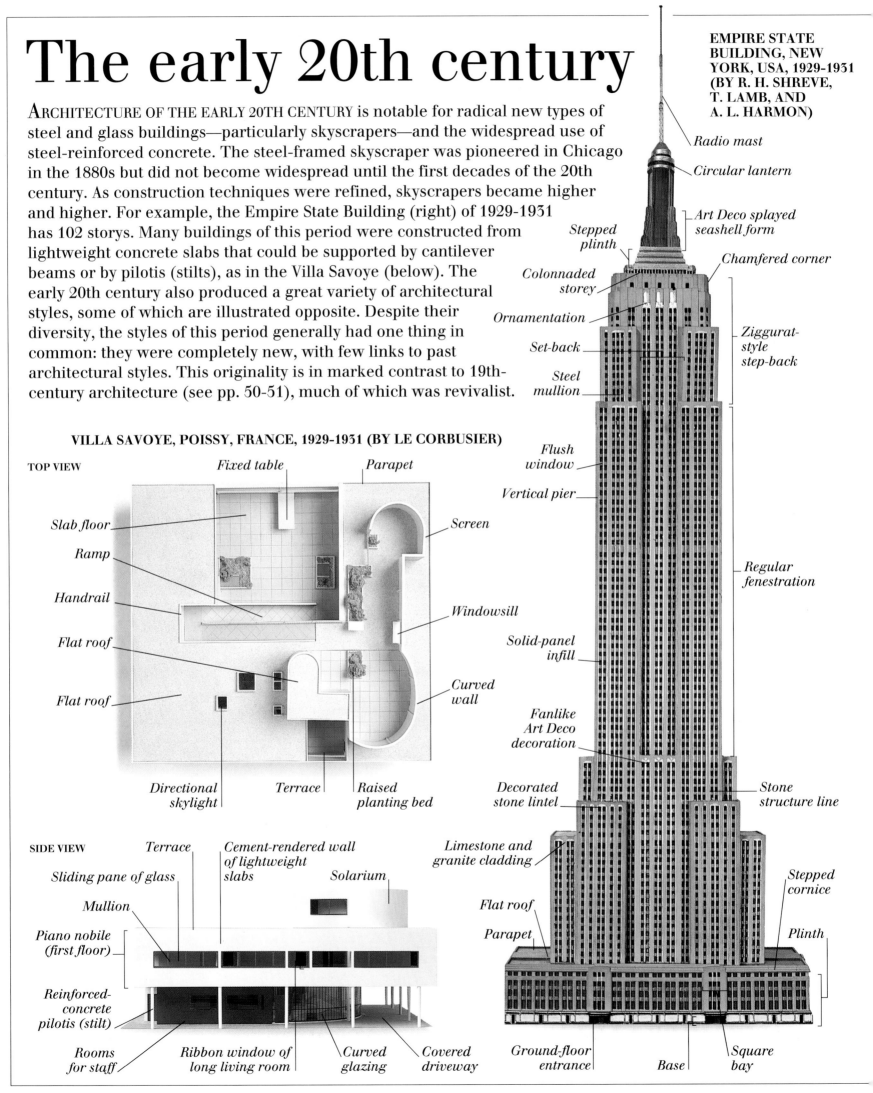

EMPIRE STATE BUILDING, NEW YORK, USA, 1929-1931 (BY R. H. SHREVE, T. LAMB, AND A. L. HARMON)

Radio mast

Circular lantern

Art Deco splayed seashell form

Stepped plinth

Chamfered corner

Colonnaded storey

Ornamentation

Ziggurat-style step-back

Set-back

Steel mullion

Flush window

Vertical pier

Regular fenestration

Solid-panel infill

Fanlike Art Deco decoration

Decorated stone lintel

Stone structure line

Limestone and granite cladding

Flat roof

Stepped cornice

Parapet

Plinth

Ground-floor entrance

Base

Square bay

VILLA SAVOYE, POISSY, FRANCE, 1929-1931 (BY LE CORBUSIER)

TOP VIEW

Fixed table

Parapet

Slab floor

Screen

Ramp

Handrail

Windowsill

Flat roof

Curved wall

Flat roof

Directional skylight

Terrace

Raised planting bed

SIDE VIEW

Terrace

Cement-rendered wall of lightweight slabs

Solarium

Sliding pane of glass

Mullion

Piano nobile (first floor)

Reinforced-concrete pilotis (stilt)

Rooms for staff

Ribbon window of long living room

Curved glazing

Covered driveway

52

MIDWAY GARDENS, CHICAGO, USA, 1914 (BY F. LLOYD WRIGHT)

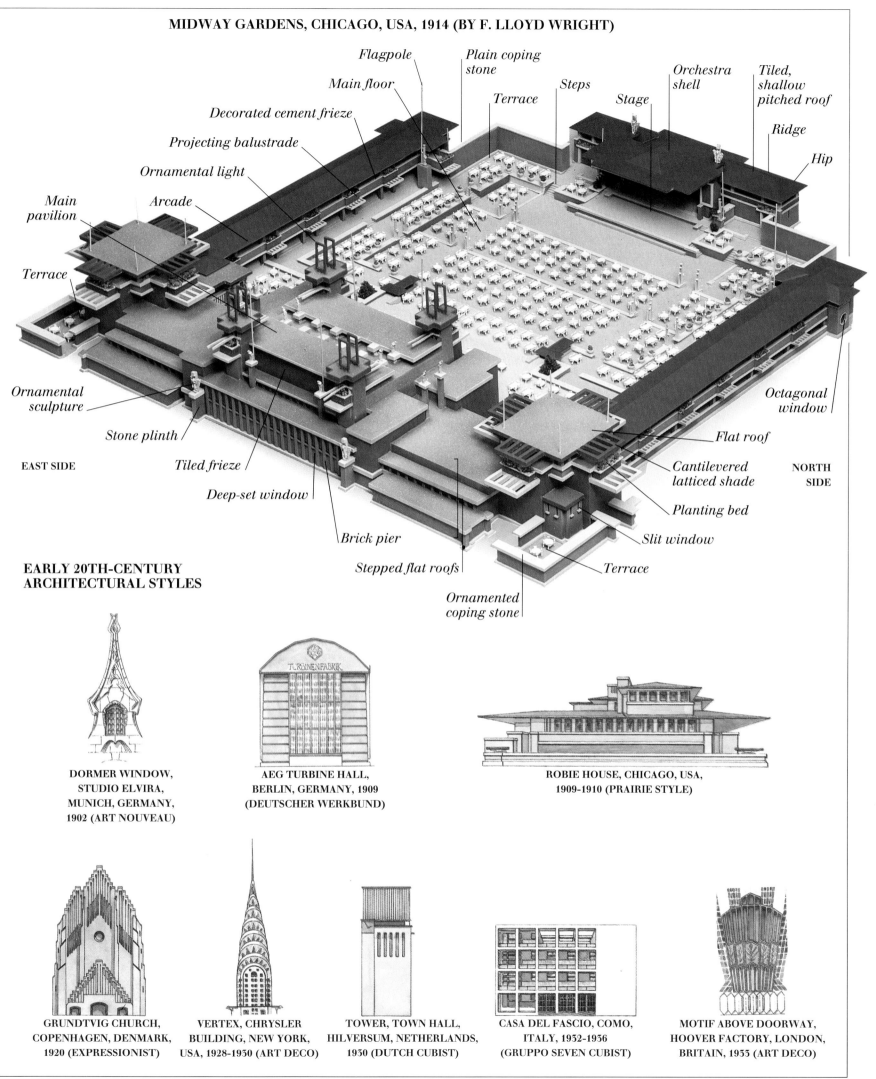

Flagpole

Plain coping stone

Main floor

Decorated cement frieze

Terrace

Steps

Stage

Orchestra shell

Tiled, shallow pitched roof

Projecting balustrade

Ridge

Ornamental light

Hip

Main pavilion

Arcade

Terrace

Octagonal window

Ornamental sculpture

EAST SIDE

Stone plinth

Tiled frieze

Flat roof

Deep-set window

Cantilevered latticed shade

NORTH SIDE

Planting bed

Brick pier

Slit window

Stepped flat roofs

Terrace

Ornamented coping stone

EARLY 20TH-CENTURY ARCHITECTURAL STYLES

DORMER WINDOW, STUDIO ELVIRA, MUNICH, GERMANY, 1902 (ART NOUVEAU)

AEG TURBINE HALL, BERLIN, GERMANY, 1909 (DEUTSCHER WERKBUND)

ROBIE HOUSE, CHICAGO, USA, 1909-1910 (PRAIRIE STYLE)

GRUNDTVIG CHURCH, COPENHAGEN, DENMARK, 1920 (EXPRESSIONIST)

VERTEX, CHRYSLER BUILDING, NEW YORK, USA, 1928-1930 (ART DECO)

TOWER, TOWN HALL, HILVERSUM, NETHERLANDS, 1930 (DUTCH CUBIST)

CASA DEL FASCIO, COMO, ITALY, 1932-1936 (GRUPPO SEVEN CUBIST)

MOTIF ABOVE DOORWAY, HOOVER FACTORY, LONDON, BRITAIN, 1933 (ART DECO)

Modern buildings 1

ARCHITECTURE SINCE ABOUT THE 1950s is generally known as modern architecture. One of its main influences has been functionalism—a belief that a building's function should be apparent in its design. Both the Centre Georges Pompidou (below and opposite) and the Hong Kong and Shanghai Bank (see pp. 56-57) are functionalist buildings. On each, elements of engineering and the building's services are clearly visible on the outside. In the 1980s, some architects rejected functionalism in favor of postmodernism, in which historical styles—particularly neoclassicism—were revived, using modern building materials and techniques. In many modern buildings, walls are made of glass or concrete hung from a frame, as in the Kawana House (right); this type of wall construction is known as curtain walling. Other modern construction techniques include the intricate interlocking of concrete vaults—as in the Sydney Opera House (see pp. 56-57)—and the use of high-tension beams to create complex roof shapes, such as the paraboloid roof of the Church of St. Pierre de Libreville (see pp. 56-57).

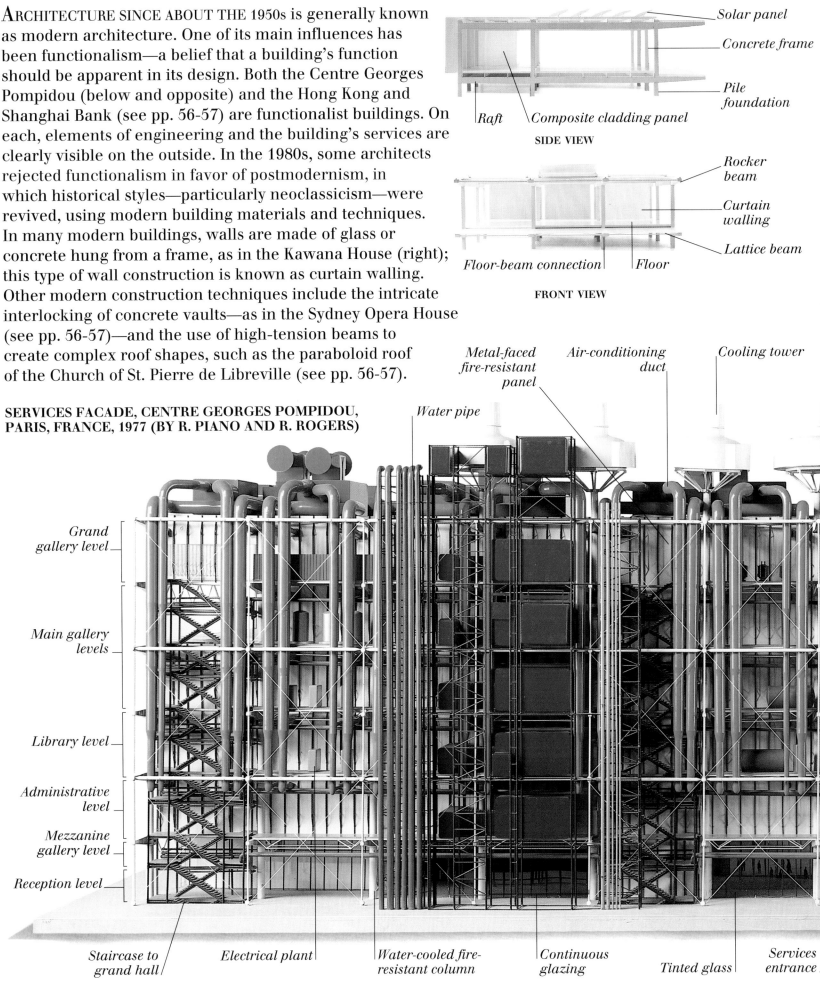

Solar panel

Concrete frame

Pile foundation

Raft   Composite cladding panel

SIDE VIEW

Rocker beam

Curtain walling

Lattice beam

Floor-beam connection   Floor

FRONT VIEW

SERVICES FACADE, CENTRE GEORGES POMPIDOU, PARIS, FRANCE, 1977 (BY R. PIANO AND R. ROGERS)

Metal-faced fire-resistant panel

Air-conditioning duct

Cooling tower

Water pipe

Grand gallery level

Main gallery levels

Library level

Administrative level

Mezzanine gallery level

Reception level

Staircase to grand hall   Electrical plant   Water-cooled fire-resistant column   Continuous glazing   Tinted glass   Services entrance

PRINCIPAL FACADE, CENTRE GEORGES POMPIDOU

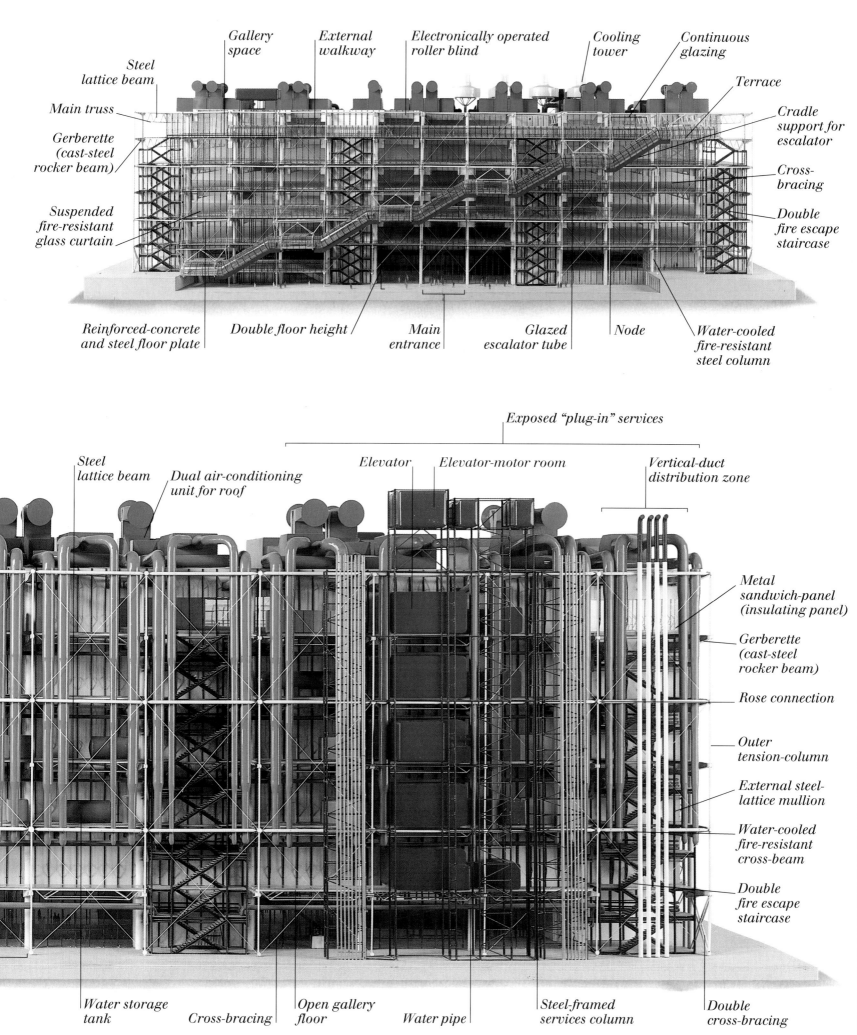

Steel lattice beam

Main truss

Gerberette (cast-steel rocker beam)

Suspended fire-resistant glass curtain

Gallery space

External walkway

Electronically operated roller blind

Cooling tower

Continuous glazing

Terrace

Cradle support for escalator

Cross-bracing

Double fire escape staircase

Reinforced-concrete and steel floor plate

Double floor height

Main entrance

Glazed escalator tube

Node

Water-cooled fire-resistant steel column

Exposed "plug-in" services

Steel lattice beam

Dual air-conditioning unit for roof

Elevator

Elevator-motor room

Vertical-duct distribution zone

Metal sandwich-panel (insulating panel)

Gerberette (cast-steel rocker beam)

Rose connection

Outer tension-column

External steel-lattice mullion

Water-cooled fire-resistant cross-beam

Double fire escape staircase

Water storage tank

Cross-bracing

Open gallery floor

Water pipe

Steel-framed services column

Double cross-bracing

Modern buildings 2

HONG KONG AND SHANGHAI BANK, HONG KONG, 1981-1985 (BY N. FOSTER)

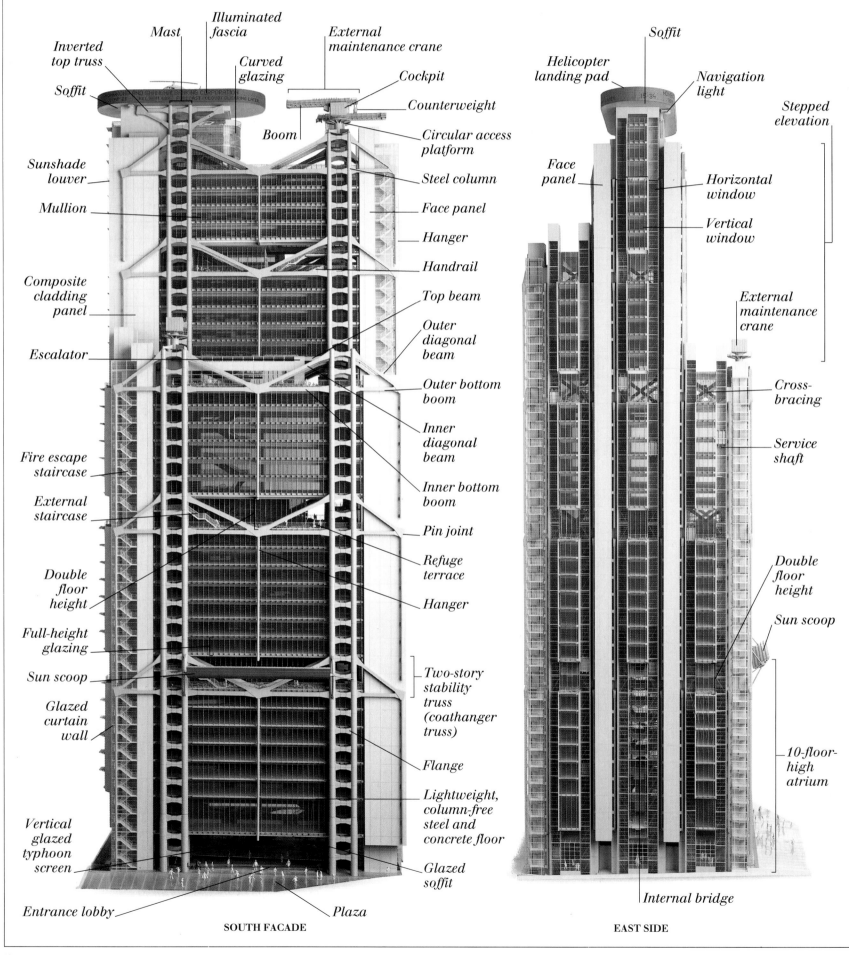

Mast

Illuminated fascia

Inverted top truss

Curved glazing

External maintenance crane

Cockpit

Soffit

Counterweight

Boom

Circular access platform

Sunshade louver

Steel column

Mullion

Face panel

Hanger

Handrail

Composite cladding panel

Top beam

Outer diagonal beam

Escalator

Outer bottom boom

Inner diagonal beam

Fire escape staircase

Inner bottom boom

External staircase

Pin joint

Double floor height

Refuge terrace

Full-height glazing

Hanger

Sun scoop

Two-story stability truss (coathanger truss)

Glazed curtain wall

Flange

Lightweight, column-free steel and concrete floor

Vertical glazed typhoon screen

Glazed soffit

Entrance lobby

Plaza

SOUTH FACADE

Soffit

Helicopter landing pad

Navigation light

Stepped elevation

Face panel

Horizontal window

Vertical window

External maintenance crane

Cross-bracing

Service shaft

Double floor height

Sun scoop

10-floor-high atrium

Internal bridge

EAST SIDE

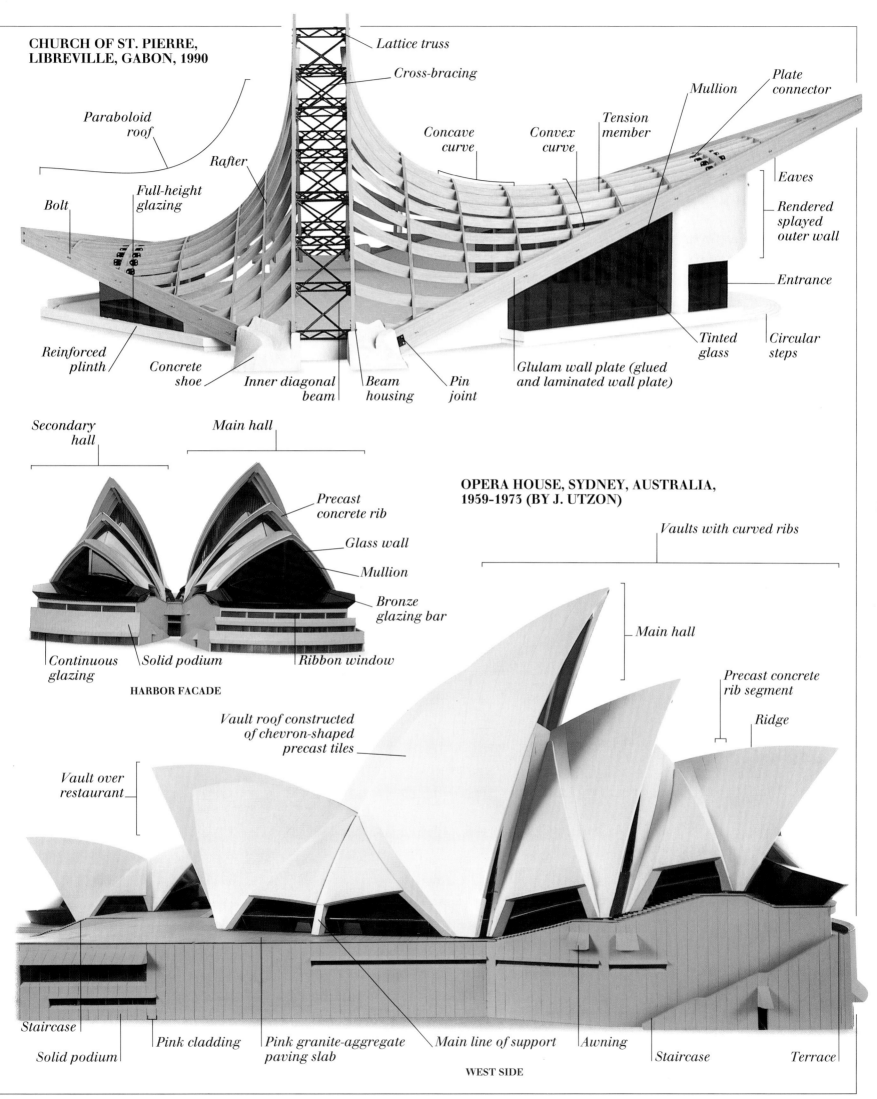

CHURCH OF ST. PIERRE, LIBREVILLE, GABON, 1990

Lattice truss

Cross-bracing

Paraboloid roof

Rafter

Concave curve

Convex curve

Tension member

Mullion

Plate connector

Full-height glazing

Eaves

Bolt

Rendered splayed outer wall

Entrance

Reinforced plinth

Concrete shoe

Inner diagonal beam

Beam housing

Pin joint

Glulam wall plate (glued and laminated wall plate)

Tinted glass

Circular steps

Secondary hall

Main hall

Precast concrete rib

OPERA HOUSE, SYDNEY, AUSTRALIA, 1959-1973 (BY J. UTZON)

Glass wall

Mullion

Bronze glazing bar

Vaults with curved ribs

Main hall

Precast concrete rib segment

Ridge

Continuous glazing

Solid podium

Ribbon window

HARBOR FACADE

Vault roof constructed of chevron-shaped precast tiles

Vault over restaurant

Staircase

Solid podium

Pink cladding

Pink granite-aggregate paving slab

Main line of support

Awning

Staircase

Terrace

WEST SIDE

57

Architectural styles

BUILDINGS CAN BE CLASSIFIED according to which of the various architectural styles they exemplify. There are three main criteria used to define a building's style: design, proportions, and ornamentation. These criteria may be influenced by various factors, including the function of a building, the materials and building techniques available, and the interests of a building's patron. The chart below shows the major architectural styles throughout the ages and across the world, with illustrations of important buildings of each style. From the chart it is possible to identify certain recurring trends, such as the importance of continuity in Far Eastern and Indian buildings, the innovative character of European architecture since medieval times, the enduring use of classical motifs, and the worldwide influence of Islamic themes.

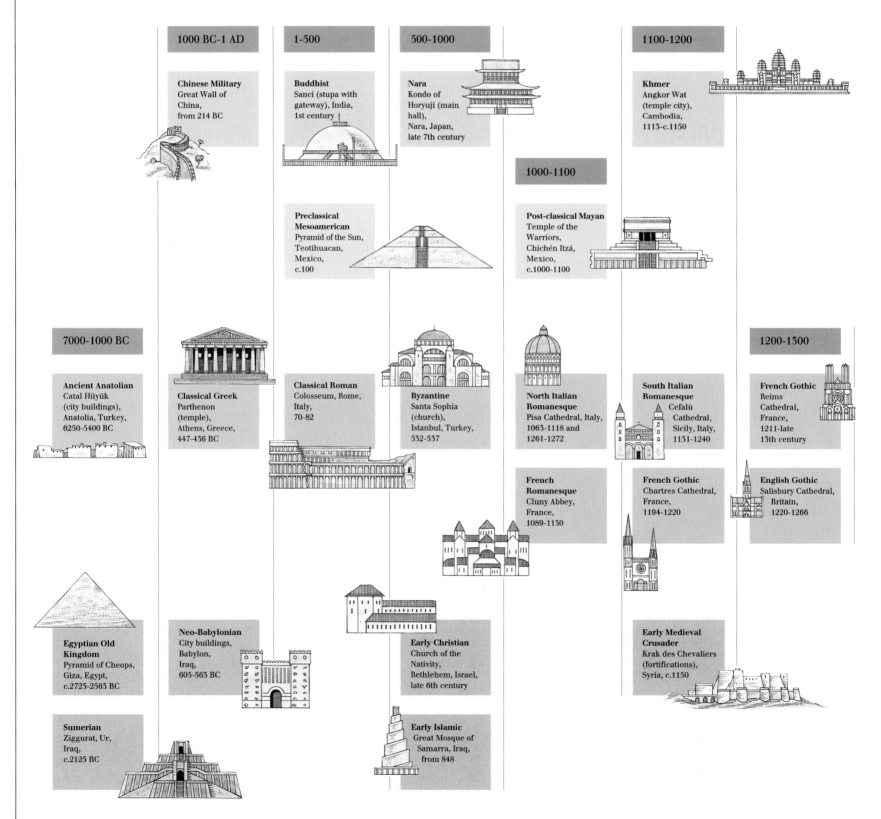

1000 BC-1 AD

Chinese Military
Great Wall of China,
from 214 BC

Buddhist
Sanci (stupa with gateway), India,
1st century

Nara
Kondo of Horyuji (main hall),
Nara, Japan,
late 7th century

1100-1200

Khmer
Angkor Wat (temple city),
Cambodia,
1113-c.1150

1-500

Preclassical Mesoamerican
Pyramid of the Sun,
Teotihuacan,
Mexico,
c.100

1000-1100

Post-classical Mayan
Temple of the Warriors,
Chichén Itzá,
Mexico,
c.1000-1100

7000-1000 BC

Ancient Anatolian
Catal Hüyük (city buildings),
Anatolia, Turkey,
6250-5400 BC

Classical Greek
Parthenon (temple),
Athens, Greece,
447-436 BC

Classical Roman
Colosseum, Rome,
Italy,
70-82

Byzantine
Santa Sophia (church),
Istanbul, Turkey,
532-537

North Italian Romanesque
Pisa Cathedral, Italy,
1063-1118 and
1261-1272

South Italian Romanesque
Cefalù Cathedral,
Sicily, Italy,
1131-1240

1200-1300

French Gothic
Reims Cathedral,
France,
1211-late
13th century

French Romanesque
Cluny Abbey,
France,
1089-1150

French Gothic
Chartres Cathedral,
France,
1194-1220

English Gothic
Salisbury Cathedral,
Britain,
1220-1266

Egyptian Old Kingdom
Pyramid of Cheops,
Giza, Egypt,
c.2723-2563 BC

Neo-Babylonian
City buildings,
Babylon,
Iraq,
605-563 BC

Early Christian
Church of the Nativity,
Bethlehem, Israel,
late 6th century

Early Medieval Crusader
Krak des Chevaliers (fortifications),
Syria, c.1150

Sumerian
Ziggurat, Ur,
Iraq,
c.2125 BC

Early Islamic
Great Mosque of Samarra, Iraq,
from 848

58

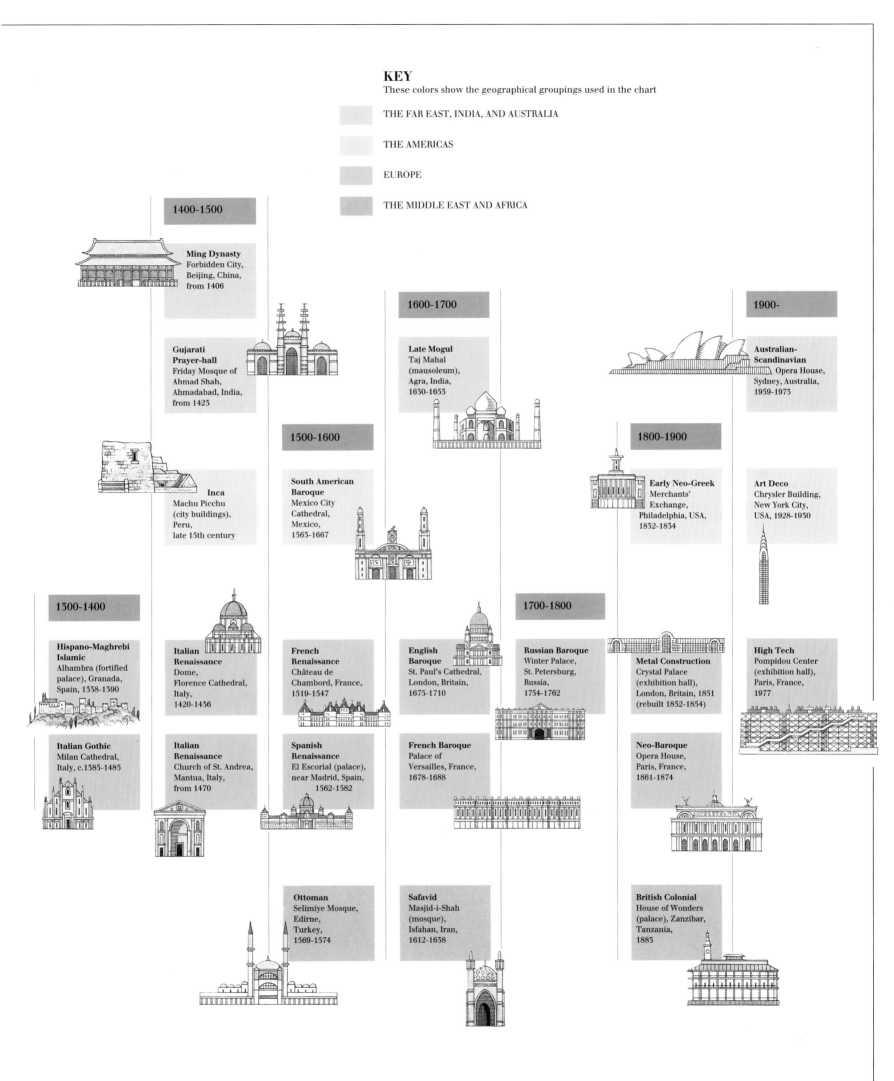

KEY
These colors show the geographical groupings used in the chart

THE FAR EAST, INDIA, AND AUSTRALIA

THE AMERICAS

EUROPE

THE MIDDLE EAST AND AFRICA

1400-1500

Ming Dynasty
Forbidden City,
Beijing, China,
from 1406

Gujarati Prayer-hall
Friday Mosque of
Ahmad Shah,
Ahmadabad, India,
from 1423

1600-1700

Late Mogul
Taj Mahal
(mausoleum),
Agra, India,
1630-1653

1900-

Australian-Scandinavian
Opera House,
Sydney, Australia,
1959-1973

Inca
Machu Picchu
(city buildings),
Peru,
late 15th century

1500-1600

South American Baroque
Mexico City
Cathedral,
Mexico,
1563-1667

1800-1900

Early Neo-Greek
Merchants'
Exchange,
Philadelphia, USA,
1832-1834

Art Deco
Chrysler Building,
New York City,
USA, 1928-1930

1300-1400

Hispano-Maghrebi Islamic
Alhambra (fortified
palace), Granada,
Spain, 1338-1390

Italian Renaissance
Dome,
Florence Cathedral,
Italy,
1420-1436

French Renaissance
Château de
Chambord, France,
1519-1547

English Baroque
St. Paul's Cathedral,
London, Britain,
1675-1710

1700-1800

Russian Baroque
Winter Palace,
St. Petersburg,
Russia,
1754-1762

Metal Construction
Crystal Palace
(exhibition hall),
London, Britain, 1851
(rebuilt 1852-1854)

High Tech
Pompidou Center
(exhibition hall),
Paris, France,
1977

Italian Gothic
Milan Cathedral,
Italy, c.1385-1485

Italian Renaissance
Church of St. Andrea,
Mantua, Italy,
from 1470

Spanish Renaissance
El Escorial (palace),
near Madrid, Spain,
1562-1582

French Baroque
Palace of
Versailles, France,
1678-1688

Neo-Baroque
Opera House,
Paris, France,
1861-1874

Ottoman
Selimiye Mosque,
Edirne,
Turkey,
1569-1574

Safavid
Masjid-i-Shah
(mosque),
Isfahan, Iran,
1612-1638

British Colonial
House of Wonders
(palace), Zanzibar,
Tanzania,
1883

Index

61

Acknowledgments

Dorling Kindersley would like to thank:
Stephen Cutler for advice and text; Gavin Morgan of the Museum of London, London; Chris Zeuner of the Weald and Downland Museum, Singleton, Sussex; Alan Hills and James Putnam of the British Museum, London; Dr Simon Penn and Michael Thomas of the Avoncroft Museum of Buildings, Bromsgrove, Worcestershire; Christina Scull of Sir John Soane's Museum, London; Paul Kennedy and John Williamson of the London Door Company, London; Lou Davis of The Original Box Sash Window Company, Windsor; Goddard and Gibbs Studios Ltd., London, for access to stained glass windows; The Royal Courts of Justice, Strand, London; Charles Brooking and Peter Dalton for access to the doors and windows in the Charles Brooking Collection, University of Greenwich, Dartford, Kent; Clare O'Brien of the Shakespeare Globe Trust, Shakespeare's Globe Museum, Bear Gardens, Southwark, London; Ken Teague of the Horniman Museum, London; Canon Haliburton, Mike Payton, Ken Stones, and Anthony Webb of St. Paul's Cathedral, London; Roy Spring of Salisbury Cathedral; Reverend Gillean Craig of the Church of St. George in the East, London; the Science Museum, London; Dr Neil Bingham; Lin Kennedy of Historic Royal Palaces; Katy Harris of Sir Norman Foster and Partners; Production Design, Thames Television plc, London, for supplying models; Dominique Reynier of Le Centre Georges Pompidou, Paris; Denis Roche of Le Musée National des Monuments Français, Paris; Franck Gioria and students at Les Compagnons du Devoir, Paris, for access to construction models; Frank Folliot of Le Musée Carnavalet, Paris; Dr Martina Harms of Hessische Landesmuseums, Darmstadt; Jefferson Chapman of the University of Tennessee, Knoxville, for access to the model of the Hypostyle Hall, Temple of Amon-Re; staff of the Palazzo Strozzi, Florence; staff of the Sydney Opera House, Sydney; staff of the Empire State Building, New York; Nick Jackson; Ann Terrell

Additional editorial assistance:
Edward Bunting, Mary Lindsay, Christine Murdock, Louise Tucker

Additional design assistance:
Alexandra Brown, Clare Shedden, Ellen Woodward

Additional photography:
Charles Brooks, Torla Evans, David Exton, Robert and Anthony Fretwell of Fretwell Photography Ltd., Lynton Gardiner, Steve Gorton, Michelangelo Gratton of Vision, Peter Hayman, Nick Nicholls, David Rudkin

Additional illustration:
Roy Flooks

Research:
Vere Dodds, Danièle Guitton, Catherine O'Rourke, Vanessa Smith

Picture credits:
Page 7 false door stelas, page 7 plant capital, page 8 Doric capital, page 8 Ionic capital, page 8 Corinthian capital, page 43 marble tomb, all British Museum. Page 53 top: Frank Lloyd Wright, American, 1867-1959, Model of Midway Gardens, 1914, executed by Richard Tickner, mixed media, 1987, 41.9 x 81.3 x 76.2 cm, 1989.48. view 1. Photograph by Robert Hashimoto. Photography courtesy of the Art Institute of Chicago

Index:
Jane Parker